# Web

# construction simplified

# OTHER TITLES BY THE SAME AUTHOR

| BP 418 | Word 95 assistant |
| BP 421 | Windows 95 assistant |
| BP 422 | Essentials of computer security |
| BP 425 | Microsoft Internet Explorer assistant |
| BP 427 | Netscape Internet Navigator assistant |
| BP 434 | PC hardware assistant |
| BP 437 | Word 97 assistant |
| BP 438 | Inside your PC |
| BP 439 | Troubleshooting your PC |
| BP 446 | How to get your PC up and running |
| BP 447 | Multimedia explained |
| BP 449 | Practical uses for your old PC |
| BP 451 | Troubleshooting your PC printer |
| BP 454 | Windows 98 assistant |
| BP 457 | Windows 98 applets explained |
| BP 458 | Tune up Windows 98 |

# OTHER TITLES OF INTEREST

| BP 403 | The Internet and World Wide Web explained |
| BP 404 | How to create web pages using HTML |
| BP 433 | Your own web site on the Internet |
| BP 441 | Creating web pages using Microsoft Office 97 |
| BP 453 | How to search the World Wide Web efficiently |
| BP 461 | Using FrontPage 98 |

# Web site construction simplified

by

Ian Sinclair

BERNARD BABANI (publishing) LTD
THE GRAMPIANS
SHEPHERDS BUSH ROAD
LONDON W6 7NF
ENGLAND

# PLEASE NOTE

Although every care has been taken with the production of this book to ensure that any projects, designs, modifications and/or programs, etc., contained herewith, operate in a correct and safe manner and also that any components specified are normally available in Great Britain, the Publishers and Author(s) do not accept responsibility in any way for the failure (including fault in design) of any project, design, modification or program to work correctly or to cause damage to any equipment that it may be connected to or used in conjunction with, or in respect of any other damage or injury that may be so caused, nor do the Publishers accept responsibility in any way for the failure to obtain specified components.

Notice is also given that if equipment that is still under warranty is modified in any way or used or connected with home-built equipment then that warranty may be void.

British Library Cataloguing in Publication Data:

A catalogue record for this book is available from the British Library

ISBN 0 85934 463 0

Cover Design by Gregor Arthur
Cover Illustration by Adam Willis
Printed and Bound in Great Britain by The Bath Press, Bath

# PREFACE

Everyone who signs up to an information provider (IP) to link up to the Internet receives an entitlement of Web space, usually free and usually around 1 Mbyte. This allows you to create your own Web site for whatever (non-commercial) purpose you want, and the facility is widely used.

You may, however, feel that this is for experts only, and some of the books that have been published in the past reinforce this view. In fact, you don't need any skills other than the usual keyboard skills, so that if you can operate a keyboard you can create a Web site.

If you are using Windows 98, you don't even need any special software tools, because Microsoft Front Page Express is an editor for Web pages that is distributed along with Windows 98. You can also create Web pages using Word 97, and if you need other software you can download it as you wish.

What you need mainly is know-how, and this book provides it by showing simple examples of design, construction, and uploading of Web pages. Also included is the important topic of how to make your Web page appear on search engines so that other users can find it.

For the really committed, a section on the HTML system of writing Web text is included, since this allows you access to more advanced forms of Web page, and also the ability to check that your page is correctly constructed.

Ian Sinclair

Autumn 1998

# ABOUT THE AUTHOR

Ian Sinclair was born in 1932 in Tayport, Fife, and graduated from the University of St. Andrews in 1956. In that year, he joined the English Electric Valve Co. in Chelmsford, Essex, to work on the design of specialised cathode-ray tubes, and later on small transmitting valves and TV transmitting tubes.

In 1966, he became an assistant lecturer at Hornchurch Technical College, and in 1967 joined the staff of Braintree College of F.E. as a lecturer. His first book, "Understanding Electronic Components" was published in 1972, and he has been writing ever since, particularly for the novice in Electronics or Computing. The interest in computing arose after seeing a Tandy TRS80 in San Francisco in 1977, and of his 180 published books, about half have been on computing topics, starting with a guide to Microsoft Basic on the TRS80 in 1979.

He left teaching in 1984 to concentrate entirely on writing, and has also gained experience in computer typesetting, particularly for mathematical texts. He has recently visited Seattle to see Microsoft at work, and to remind them that he has been using Microsoft products longer than most Microsoft employees can remember.

# ACKNOWLEDGEMENTS

I would like to thank the staff of Text 100 Ltd. for providing the Windows 98 software which is so frequently mentioned in the course of this book. I would also like to acknowledge the vast bank of useful information held on various Web sites and comments made in News group notes. I would like to also acknowledge the help of Global Internet Ltd. and Terrapin Internet Ltd.

# TRADEMARKS

Microsoft, MS-DOS, Windows, Windows 98, NT, FrontPage and FrontPage Express are either registered trademarks or trademarks of Microsoft Corporation.

All other brand and product names used in this book are recognised as trademarks, or registered trademarks, of their respective companies.

# CONTENTS

**1 Your own Web site** .................................................. 1
  Web sites ............................................................. 1
  Terms .................................................................... 2
  HTML ................................................................... 4
  Creating HTML ..................................................... 6
  Uploading ............................................................. 9
  Maintaining the site .............................................. 9

**2 Designing a Web page** ........................................... 11
  What is a Web page? ............................................ 11
  Aims and objectives ............................................ 12
  Text headings ..................................................... 13
  Pictures .............................................................. 15
  Sounds ............................................................... 18
  Hyperlinks .......................................................... 18

**3 WYSIWYG software** ............................................ 19
  Software ............................................................. 19
  **FrontPage Express** ......................................... 19
    Starting an index page ...................................... 22
    Working with text ............................................. 26
    Graphics .......................................................... 31
    Tables .............................................................. 32
    Table alterations .............................................. 34
    Cell properties ................................................. 37
    Other formatting .............................................. 39
    Other page properties ....................................... 40
    Other inserts .................................................... 41
  **Using Word** .................................................... 45
    Word Tables ..................................................... 49
    Word graphics .................................................. 50
    Link insertion .................................................. 51
  **AOLpress** ....................................................... 51
    Starting work ................................................... 52
    Starting your own page ...................................... 54
    Page colours and backgrounds ........................... 56
    Links ............................................................... 57

Styles ....................................................................58
Character styles...................................................59
List and table options.......................................59
Pictures ...............................................................62
Image manipulation ..........................................63
**Amaya**..................................................................**64**
Browsing..............................................................65
Text.......................................................................66
Pictures ...............................................................69
Links....................................................................70
Removing a link or a target ..........................71
**4 Creating your Web page**.................................**73**
File locations ....................................................73
**Using FPE other templates** ...........................**75**
Normal page .......................................................77
**Using Word or other WPs** ..............................**78**
**Using plain text**.................................................**80**
Preparing text....................................................81
HTML editors.....................................................83
Adding other items...........................................87
**5 Uploading and changing** ...............................**89**
Case sensitivity.................................................89
**Save As** ................................................................**90**
**FTP** .......................................................................**91**
Browsing and file transfer .............................91
**Web Publishing Wizard**...................................**94**
**Using Terrapin FTP**..........................................**96**
Terrapin uploading ...........................................97
Site maintenance................................................100
**Other FTPs** ........................................................**101**
WS_FTP...............................................................103
**6 Making it known**............................................**107**
**Searching**............................................................**107**
**Search engines** ...................................................**108**
Using Submit-It!...............................................112
**Checking for your entry** .................................**114**

**7 HTML guide** ................................................... **115**

Elements and tags ..................................... **116**

Head and body .......................................... **117**

Looking at a file........................................ **118**

**Tag list** ................................................... **119**

Body tags .................................................. **119**

Lists ......................................................... **120**

**Text character effects** .................................. **124**

Logical styles list........................................ **125**

Physical styles list...................................... **125**

Escape Sequences ...................................... **125**

**Links** ..................................................... **126**

Named anchors .......................................... **128**

**Images** ................................................... **129**

**Image links** ............................................. **131**

Backgrounds ............................................. **131**

Thumbnails ............................................... **132**

Tables ...................................................... **133**

**Forms** .................................................... **134**

**Appendix** ................................................ **135**

A hit counter.............................................. **135**

**INDEX** ................................................... **137**

# 1 Your own Web site

## Web sites

Some of the Web sites that you see are the all-singing, all-dancing efforts that belong to large commercial organisations or to people who earn a living from the Web. You would expect these to be impressive, and they usually are. Other sites, however, are more modest. They are created by ordinary PC users who want to make contacts, to share views or knowledge, to show you what they have achieved or what they want to achieve. These sites will use text, perhaps some pictures, possibly sounds, and a few hyperlinks to other sites that the site designer finds interesting.

The theme of this book is that you do not need special knowledge or skills, and in particular, programming ability, to create such a simple Web site for yourself. Providing you can type or copy text, and obtain any illustrations you want in a standard graphics format, then you too can create your own Web site, and all you need is a little know-how. Whatever you may have heard about the need to understand HTML or to be able to program in the Java language you can forget — one of the problems about the Net is that so much advice about complications is so soon out of date.

In this book, we'll look at how to create a simple Web site using ordinary word-processor methods, with software that you probably have already, and with some co-operation from your Internet IP (Information Provider). Anyone who signs up to a provider nowadays can expect to be allocated some space for a Web site. This is often 1 Mbyte, but several providers, notably Global Internet, now provide a generous 20 Mbyte. This is more than most users need, and a simple site need use only a fraction of a 1 Mbyte allocation.

As an example, my own site was created using the methods that are described in this book. Take a look at:

# Web site construction simplified

http://www.users.globalnet.co.uk/~iansin

to see what I am describing and to see if what appears there looks like the type of site that you might want to make for yourself.

## Terms

Before we start, we need to make sure that we are speaking the same language. If the following terms are already familiar to you, please read the next section. If they are not, please note well, because we shall be using them throughout this book.

**Path** means the set of folders that you have to browse through to get to a file, either on your hard drive or on a remoter server. The separation of folders and files is shown using backslash marks, so that:

C:\Data\Myfiles\MyWeb\index.htm

shows that the file index.htm is in a folder called *MyWeb*, which is in a folder called *Myfiles*, which is turn is in a folder called *Data* on the hard drive C:. The illustration shows this path would appear viewed in Windows Explorer — note that the path is printed in the *Address line*.

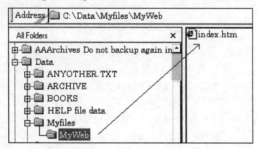

- Do not confuse the use of backslash marks used in a path with the forward slashes used in URL names.

**IP** (Information Provider) is the company whose computer you contact to make connection with the Web. Most users

2

will make contact using a modem and a telephone number that the IP has allocated, and you will have set up Windows Dial-Up Networking (DUN) so that your user name and password will be entered automatically when you make contact. Competition among IPs is intense, and you can expect nowadays to get unlimited Internet access for less than £100 per year, or even free if you use some of the networks that carry advertising.

**URL** (Uniform Resource Locator) is a form of address used for Web sites, usually starting with http://www.

**Server** means a large computer used by an IP to hold Internet files. A machine of this size will not use Windows and is much more likely to use an operating system called **Unix**. This imposes some conditions on items such as your filenames which will be explained later.

**Hyperlink** is the name given to a feature that makes a net document so very different from one on paper. A Hyperlink consists of a piece of text or a picture which is distinguished from the rest by being coloured or with a coloured underline or border. Clicking with the mouse on this hyperlink (often just called a *link*) will take you to another part of the document, a different document, even a different Web site.

**Text editor** is a program like Windows NotePad that stores text using one memory byte for each character. This system, called ASCII or text-file, does not permit any formatting to be stored.

**Word processor** means a large and elaborate program that can create and store formatted text, usually with tables and pictures. The files contain a large number of formatting codes along with the usual ASCII codes for the text.

**Upload** means copy a file on your hard drive (or any other local file) to the Web server.

3

## Web site construction simplified

**Download** means to copy a file or folder on the Web server to your local hard drive.

**ToolTips** are a useful feature of Windows programs, and if they are enabled, as they ought to be, you will see a small panel of explanatory text appear, after a short delay, when you place the pointer over a tool icon. No labelled lists of tool icons appear in this book because you can find the action of each icon from the ToolTips.

## HTML

The Internet has developed by using the efforts of a large number of people, and in the very early days, only text files could be interchanged. This was done using the universal ASCII code in which all the letters of the English alphabet, along with digits and punctuation marks, are represented by numbers in the range 32 to 127. This is a simple system which does not allow for accented letters, shapes, different type fonts or sizes, but it has the great advantage of being concise, and when we had to work at very slow communication rates, a concise file was a great advantage.

Word-processors have always used more elaborate codes so that they could produce the effects that are impossible using ASCII text files, but the size of files that programs such as Word will produce, even from a very short text file, are much too large to send easily over the Internet, taking too long to transmit and taking up too much space on the host computer.

Several ways of making such files more compact have been invented, and in addition, ways of using ASCII code numbers only, since these codes use only 7/8 of one byte each, and the spare parts can be used up by compressing the files, making them shorter. There is no space in this book to go into the fascinating history of the methods that have been used (some of which are still used) for sending formatted documents using ASCII codes, but we need to know

4

something about the one that is particularly relevant and important, HyperText Markup Language or HTML.

It's not so ferocious as it sounds. The idea, which it shares with several similar systems, is to use ASCII codes only for the text, and to devise combinations of ASCII characters for effects like bold or italic, different fonts and sizes, foreign characters and so on. The code letters are put between angle brackets, so that, for example, <H1> means that what follows is in the style that is used for the most important headings, the level-1 headings. Keeping with this example, </H1> turns off the effect, so that only the text between these marks <H1> and </H1> is in the heading-1 style.

That is simple enough, and what makes a Web page in HTML look so difficult to understand is that so many other effects are coded with these angle-bracket signs — if you don't know the codes you cannot type directly in HTML.

Fortunately, that is a problem that has been overcome, and you can nowadays design and produce your Web pages without any knowledge of HTML. If you want to go further and dig deeper into Web production, then it's useful to learn HTML, but for most users this will never be needed. For those who need to know or would like to know, the chapter headed *HTML guide* provides a useful introduction.

There are four main steps in creating your Web site:

1. Planning. This is the most important and the most neglected aspect. Without planning your site is haphazard, possibly unreadable. The most important aspect is deciding what goes into the main page (the *index page*) and what is consigned to other pages.

2. Writing the text and so creating HTML files. This, contrary to what you might expect, is the easiest part.

3. Uploading the files. There are several ways of doing this, and you may be able simply to use a *Save As*

command in the software you have used to create the text.

4. Maintaining the site. You need to be sure that information is kept up to date, so that all of your files will need to be renewed at intervals. This may require you to upload new files or modify the files that you have uploaded. You may need additional software for this.

## Creating HTML

Assuming that you don't know any HTML codes and don't particularly want to, what software is available to help you to create a Web page? There is a choice, which is:

1. Editors of the WYSIWYG type.

2. HTML editors with automatic code insertion.

3. Word processors that create HTML files.

4. Text editors along with HTML converters.

The first type of editor allows you to type text and format it, so that what you see is pretty well what you get, as the initials suggest. Editors of this type can also insert special effects such as check boxes and radio buttons and, of course, hypertext links, and save the lot as an HTML file on your hard drive or save it directly in the same format to your Web server. You have the option of seeing either the text as you typed it, or the HTML code. Microsoft FrontPage Express, supplied with Windows 98, is a cut-down version of a much more elaborate program of this type, called Microsoft Front Page 98.

There are several other programs of this type, and some suites of programs, such as Lotus SmartSuite, incorporate HTML creation. Several makes of computers bundle this software, so that many users have access to these HTML creating actions. In additions, there are excellent WYSIWYG editors that you can download, some of which are entirely free. Popular WYSIWYG editors available free on the Web include Amaya and AOLpress.

If you already have and use Windows 98, consider learning the use of FrontPage Express , since it is built-in and easy to use. Since the Help files of FrontPage Express are not really helpful, the use of this program will be illustrated in detail throughout this book because it is typical of most other WYSIWYG editors.

• The more elaborate WYSIWYG editors incorporate spell-checking, and if you look at the spelling on many Web pages you will see that the addition of this action is a very useful one.

A very different approach is followed by the type of editors that are listed as HTML editors. This type of editor creates HTML code directly, and this is also what you see on the screen. You do not need to know the codes for yourself, however, because the editor allows you to click the effect you want and type the text that goes with it, so that the codes are added automatically. HotDog is one of the best-known examples of this type, and you can download it from the Web and try it free for 30 days.

The advantage of this type of editor is that it is much smaller and faster than the WYSIWYG, an advantage if you are downloading the software slowly at an expensive time of day or if your hard drive space is limited. In addition, as you use an editor of this type you will be learning HTML coding, and this is very useful if your aims are to become really proficient in Web site creation.

Another approach is the use of a word processor that can save files in HTML format, and which has Web page Wizards. Word 8.0 (Word 97) is in this class, and if you installed it with the option of *Web Page Authoring* enabled, you will be able to create Web pages directly with Word. Even if you do not use the Authoring Wizard, you can still type your text in Word, check it for spelling and, perhaps, grammar, and then save the file in HTML format.

If you have Word, you will already have some experience of its text handling, so that you have much less to learn if you want to use it for Web page creation. Even if you do not use Word for your Web files, it's an advantage to use it for preparing text for FrontPage Express, because Word, unlike FrontPage Express, can spell-check your pages, and show in a *Print Preview* roughly what they will look like. In addition, when you have saved a file in HTML form, you can click on the file in Explorer to get a view of it as you will see it in the Explorer browser.

- This is useful, because despite all efforts for standardisation, not all browsers will show a Web page in the same way. If your page looks good in Explorer 4.0, then a majority of Internet users will be able to read it.

The last option is a low-cost way to HTML code if you have an old version of Word or other word-processor that cannot work with HTML files. If you create your text using such applications, making use of their formatting and spell-checking actions, you can use software for HTML conversion to create and save the HTML codes. You can even convert plain ASCII text to HTML and then incorporate formatting effects into the HTML files. Software of this type is widely available on the Net.

- You can also download software that will convert HTML files into text files so that older text editors and word-processors can work with the HTML files that you get from the Net.

- Remember always that what you create may not look as you intended it when it is viewed by another browser. You should always check work by looking at the HTML files locally, using your own browser, and also by contacting your own Web site when the files have been transferred.

## Uploading

Once you have designed and constructed your Web page or pages, you need to upload them to the memory space that has been assigned to you by your Internet provider. Each different IP will have different methods, but typically, you will have to activate your Web space by typing a Web address, possibly the address that you will use. For example, you can activate your Web space if you have a Global connection by going to the address:

http://www.global.net/uk/home/support/webspace/

and other providers will use similar methods. You should be able to find this out either from the documents that your IP has sent you or from the IP's home page.

Once your Web site has been activated you can start uploading files to it. Your set of files must contain one that the IP software can identify as the main file, and the usual convention is that this file must be called *index.htm* or *index.html*. This main file should contain hyperlinks to the other files, or to a file that in turn links to others. This point is so important that it will be repeated several times in this book.

- You should use only lower-case lettering, no capitals, for your filenames. The reason for this will be discussed later.

## Maintaining the site

Unless your site contains only historical data it will need to be updated at intervals. The best scheme for doing this is to keep the files locally on your hard drive and review them now and again. When you feel that a file looks its age you can update the information and save it to your hard drive. At intervals, you can copy these updated files to your Web site. This may be possible using the software that you used to create the site, but you are likely to find that FTP software is much easier to use and more convenient.

FTP (file transfer protocol) software is primarily intended for copying (downloading) software from remote sites, and it is not so well-known as it used to be because browsers like Microsoft Internet Explorer 4.0 can also carry out this action. What make FTP software useful is that it works faster, and it allows you to see a list of the files and folders on the remote site as if they were on your own hard drive. Some FTP programs even allow you to drag and drop files as if they were all on your own hard drive.

- In addition, they allow you to delete files that are on the Web site, something that a browser cannot do.

# 2 Designing a Web page

## What is a Web page?

You might think that you know what a Web page is by now, but it helps if we can get the idea really clear. To start with, a Web page is the contents of a file. It might just be a few lines on the screen, or it might be a chunk of text and pictures that needed scrolling and would need several pages of paper to print out. Whatever its size, if it is contained in a single file it is one single Web page. The illustration shows part of my own home page as it appears in Internet Explorer 4.0.

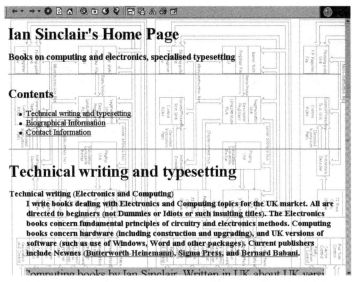

You can, if you like, keep all your information on one single Web page. This is particularly useful if you haven't much to say or show, and if you are sure that you will never need to add much. You will see many pages like this on the Net, and there is nothing wrong with the principle. If the page is a long one, you can use a short set of headings at the start with hyperlinks to the different sections of the page.

## Web site construction simplified

For many users, however, it make sense to split up what you have to say into different pages. One advantage of this is that you can keep the main (*index*) page unchanged and just extend and update the other pages. Another point is that you are likely to have several sections of data (your biography, your interests, your family photos, etc.) and you might want to keep these on separate pages so that anyone who is browsing your page can get to material of interest quickly and equally easily avoid material that is not of interest.

You do not have to make your mind up at first, but you should always start Web page design by thinking how you would divide up the material. Take a critical look at other Web sites — some are models of neat design, others are ramshackle constructions with information scattered around and difficult to read. Always remember that however simple your first Web page may be, you will almost certainly want to change it later. If this can be done easily, that's a great incentive to keep the site updated and looking interesting.

Another important point concerns the words you use in your main index page, because these are the words that a search engine will find. If, for example, you want your page to turn up in any search for the words *technical drawing* and *mechanical engineering*, you must make certain that these appear early in your index page. You might want to make your first paragraph one that is constructed from these indexing words. If you do so, these words will appear in the synopsis that many search engines show for each Web site.

## Aims and objectives

Like any publication, you should start outlining your Web page with main headings. It will help you a lot if you have a word processor that is capable of outlining, as all the main ones can. At this point, don't worry about how the final Web page will look, because it's more important at this stage to outline what you have to say to the world.

Outline headings are much easier if you can decide what you want your Web site to do. Is it to advertise that you can provide services such as making perfect scale models, writing CV's, criticising TV programmes, or using some other talent? By contrast, are you just looking for people with similar interests to share information? Have you amassed information on some topic that is of great interest to you but which no publisher deems worthy of printing? Do you think the story of your life so far might be interesting or inspiring to others?

Once you can determined aims and objectives like this you are well on the way to making a useful outline. This can, incidentally, be done using FrontPage Express (as we'll see later) but it's much better done using a word processor because you can carry out spell-checking and outlining much more easily with a good word processor.

- You can make just as effective an outline on paper, but you have to be prepared to use several sheets so that you can try out different arrangements.

Once you have the main items of your outline in place, print them on paper and read them critically. You might want to change text or alter the positions of headings, and it's all easy at this stage. With a good outliner program, you can make changes at any stage, but remember that once you have converted your text into HTML format for your Web site, it is rather more difficult to alter things like the order of headings and their text. Unless you are very short of time, take a good look at it now.

## Text headings

Your outline now provides you with your main text headings, and it's time now to start filling in detail. For some items, you may want a large number of sub-headings. For example, if the main heading is *My life so far*, you might want to put in subheadings such as *My parents*, *My early*

# Web site construction simplified

*life*, *School days*, *Entering adulthood*, *My working life* and so on. The illustration shows how some of this might appear if you used the Outline View of Word.

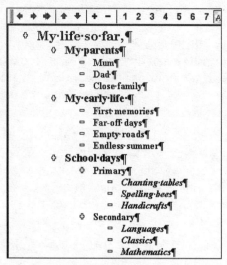

Some forms of outline might call for a list or table. If you want to proclaim your abilities in model-making, you might want to list all the models that you have made, and you will have to decide whether to list in order of creation, alphabetical title order, or some other order. If your work consists of water-colour paintings that have been sold, you might want to construct a table of titles and buyers, possibly of prices paid, to show off your talent.

If a portion of your page consists of sincerely-held views, you might like to develop the arguments both for **and** against your viewpoint — this avoids the unpleasant fanaticism that creeps into pages that show total blind support for some theory or belief (the dafter the belief, the more passionate and abusive the text appears to be).

Again, this calls for organisation using sub-headings, and some time spent reading your work critically. Always read from a paper copy, because few people seem to be able to cope with critical reading of material on screen, possibly because it is not possible to look quickly back and ahead on the small area of a screen.

## Pictures

Some Web pages require no pictures, but most can be enriched by the addition of some graphical material. The requirement is obvious if you are trumpeting your artistic talents to the world, but even if your work is more splash than sketch you can probably make your site more appealing if you use graphics.

The use of graphics is not equally easy for all users. Anyone equipped with a scanner can convert photographs into the form of a drawing file, and these should then be edited and saved as either GIF or JPG files.

The JPG format is particularly compact and ideally suited to the Web, but you should keep a copy in some other format as well, using the JPG version in your site only. The reason is that JPG is a *lossy* format — if you load a JPG file into a drawing program and edit it, then save again, some detail will vanish each time you do this. If you keep a copy in another format, editing will not cause any unintentional losses and you can save the changed drawing in JPG form for your Web site.

If you do not have a scanner and could make good use of one, consider buying one now that prices of good-quality colour scanners are so low. At one time, a monochrome scanner was an expensive extra, justified only if you carried out a large amount of graphical work. Nowadays, a scanner or a combined printer/copier/scanner is a familiar part of a complete package, and adding a scanner is not something that will break the budget.

One point to watch is the size of files. Even a modest GIF file in colour can take 180,000 bytes of space, and this also imposes a penalty in terms of the time it will take to

15

download. Some sites are littered with graphics effects, and the result is that you can spend several minutes waiting for something that makes not a shred of difference to the amount of information that you get from the page. Commercial Web sites are guilty of this, creating giant coloured lettering or logos as picture files, and for that reason your Web browser provides the option of ignoring all pictures. How would your Web site look when contacted by a browser that was configured to ignore pictures?

Considering that point, use graphics carefully, and always include a title. When such material is browsed using the no-graphics option, the title will appear, and the viewer will see a box with an icon in place of the picture. If the title is descriptive, the viewer can then decide whether or not to right-click the icon and take the *Show picture* option that overrules the browser and downloads that picture. Your rendering of *Me and my cat* will be of interest to some, and others will thank you for not wasting their time.

- Another approach is to use graphics only in separate pages, so that the reader has to click on a link in the main index page to see the pictures. This allows the main page to download quickly

If you need graphics and do not have a scanner, you have to consider what sort of graphics to use. If you must include photographs you can take your photos to any computing bureau that includes a scanning service (a local newspaper will either do this for you or point you to someone who can). There are postal services, but you should not send precious pictures through the post to someone you do not know unless you have back-up copies. The files will usually be delivered back to you on a floppy — a point that limits the size of files unless a Zip format is used. Remember that a photo taken by someone else may be subject to copyright.

You may be able to illustrate your page using drawings made by CAD or painting packages. Modern CAD programs are very capable, and will handle 3D and colour, and there are also the painting packages of which Microsoft Paint is packaged with Windows (95 or 98). If you use CAD, you need to be able to save your drawing in a form that can be placed into your Web page, and this means GIF or JPG, certainly not the native format of the drawing program or the DXF format that is used to allow CAD programs to read each others creations.

If you use a painting program, it should be able to work with GIF and JPG files. The most recent version of Windows Paint (98) will save and load using these formats, but only if some part of Microsoft Office has been installed so as to provide graphics converter programs. You may, however, be able to download suitable converter programs.

If you use graphics to anything more than a very occasional extent, you should consider obtaining a modern version of the Paint Shop Pro software. This is often packaged in time-limited form on magazine CD-ROMs, and this gives you an opportunity to find out how useful this software is for any form of graphics work. Apart from anything else, it allows you to convert from most formats into the desired GIF and JPG types that you need for the Web.

- If you use graphics on an everyday basis, you probably already have a package such as Corel that will deal with any type of pictures that you want to use. If your needs are less exacting, you need not go so far, but you might find that an older version of the Corel suite (such as CorelDraw! 4.0) does all that you need, and much more, for a remarkably low price.

- One important point you need to know is that HTML files do not **contain** graphics, only links to graphics. This keeps the HTML file short, and allows for the option to view without seeing graphics

# Web site construction simplified

Video on a Web page is not so common for non-commercial users, and it has the disadvantage of using a large amount of storage space and requiring a long time to download. Never make a video clip part of your index page, because the long downloading time will make many people who are browsing decide to stop the download prematurely. If you feel that you need to include video, make this part of a separate page that is downloaded when the viewer clicks a link on your index page. This way, the viewer is prepared for the large download and accepts that a video is being sent.

## Sounds

Sound is still not so common on Web sites as graphics, mainly because sound does not carry the sort of information that the Web page needs. You also need more hardware and software for sound than for text. In addition, short bursts of sound require a large amount of Web space and a long download time, second only to video. If sound is an essential part of your life, then say this in your index page and use a link to a page that contains your sound clips. Remember that a sound clip may also be subject to copyright.

## Hyperlinks

If you have browsed over other people's pages, you will know that a hyperlink is a piece of text or an icon that can be clicked to move viewing to another page, another part of the same page, or to another Web site. The use of hyperlinks makes it easy to break up your work into sections, and you can also provide a list of links to other Web sites that you like, saving the user the need to type in names to the browser.

# 3 WYSIWYG software

## Software

Good software is important to aid you to create a Web site, just as it is for word processing, creating spreadsheets or database and all other computing activities. One of the encouraging features of Web software is that much of it has been developed for non-commercial uses (such as for academic uses) so that is can be downloaded free, or at low shareware prices. If you have in the past equated freeware or shareware with half-baked programs, it's time to reconsider — after all, even the major browsers are freeware.

You should look carefully, using Windows Explorer, at the folders on the CD that your IP will have sent you so that you could make your first Net connection. This CD will almost certainly be packed with useful material, both text files of advice and folders with Net and other utilities. You are quite likely to find some programs that are mentioned in this book, such as HotDog, and others that can be very useful in developing a Web site. If you do not want to use the software that has been provided in this way, search for other software using your browser. There is no shortage of software, all that you need is time to download the stuff that looks interesting and to try it out.

## FrontPage Express

FrontPage Express is an application from Microsoft, and is packaged along with Internet Explorer 4.0 and therefore also with Windows 98. If you have either, or both, of these, you should be able to find FrontPage Express, though you may not have installed it when you first installed the main software. If you do not find a folder called FrontPage Express in your *Program Files* folder, you will need to go back to your CD-ROM Setup program to add this item to your collection. If you did not install FrontPage Express

# Web site construction simplified

along with Windows 98, you can use the Control Panel — Add/Remove Software item to add this software.

- FrontPage Express is a cut-down version of a much more powerful program called FrontPage 98. If you subsequently want to create much more elaborate Web pages, your experience with this simplified version will allow you to transfer easily to using FrontPage 98.

FrontPage Express is a typical example of the WYSIWYG type of Web page creation software. It behaves very much like a simple text editor — you don't have to know anything about HTML codes. All you need to do is to pick a suitable template, point and click, and type text. Since FrontPage Express comes from the Microsoft stable you will find it very similar to WordPad and Microsoft Word as far as creating a document is concerned.

One difference, however, is very important. You need to type text directly, or import your formatted text into FrontPage Express. If you use cut/copy and paste you **must** cut or copy the text from an ASCII text editor such as Notepad. If, for example, you cut text from Word and paste it into FrontPage Express, you will find that what appears in FrontPage Express is HTML code, not plain text. If you want to prepare your text in a formatting word-processor, you should not transfer it by using cut/copy and paste. The way to import such text is to save it as a word-processor file, and then use the Insert — File menu of FrontPage Express, selecting the option of *Normal Text* when you are asked what form of text it is.

- You might consider using one of the improved versions of NotePad, such as Cetus Notepad (downloaded from the Net) which incorporates a spelling checker, if you want to use Cut and Paste for your editing.

To start FrontPage Express for the first time, you can use Start — Programs — Internet Explorer —FrontPage Express but you will find it much easier if you drag a shortcut from the folder:

C:\Program Files\Microsoft FrontPage Express\BIN

to the fast-launch tray (next to the Start button) or to the Desktop or to another part of the Start menu. The program name is FPXPRESS.EXE.

When the program starts, it looks like this:

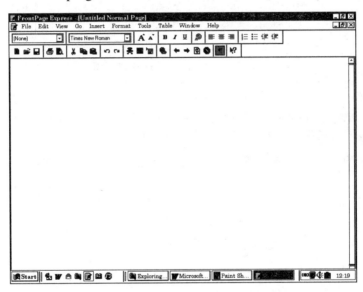

and the menu (top line) is very similar to those of WordPad and Word.

The menu line contains File, Edit, View, Go, Insert, Format, Tools, Tables, Windows and Help. Of these, the Help menu is of very little practical assistance, because the Help index makes use of just a few pages that do not go into details of how to achieve anything. The main menu actions are available also from icons, and for simple page construction, you do not need to use more than a handful of icons.

## Web site construction simplified

FrontPage Express allows for the construction of quite elaborate pages, but you should avoid trying to use these advanced features while you are learning to construct a page. In particular, the use of WebBots may not be supported by your IP, so that incorporating such components in your text may cause problems. Several other types of inserts need knowledge of how the Web space will deal with them, and some may require code to be written for such purposes as filling in forms on-line. We'll avoid these actions which are, in any case, not needed for a simple page.

There are two main ways of constructing your Web page using FrontPage Express. One is to make use of a ready-made template, and this is particularly suitable for your first effort at a Web page. The other is to import a file from a word processor, and this can be particularly useful for supplementary pages (not the index page).

### Starting an index page

You can start your index page by running FrontPage Express and clicking click File — New. You will see a list of templates and Wizards appear.

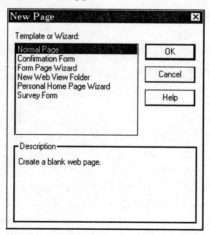

The first of these is *Normal Page*, which is useful for creating add-on pages linked to your index page, but for your index page you should click on *Personal Home Page Wizard*, which will create an outline of an index page for you.

When you select the Wizard, the first step is a display of main sections of the page, as illustrated here:

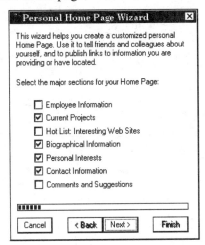

For your first effort you should make this as simple as possible. You might, for example, select *Current Projects*, *Biographical Information*, *Personal Interests* and *Contact Information* from the seven options that are presented.

Each choice you make in this list will create a separate section of your page that you can add to with text, and each section will be bookmarked so that it can be reached easily by clicking an index of hyperlinks. The hyperlinks are indicated in the usual way with blue lettering, and the bookmarks are shown with dotted blue underlining when the page is complete.

When you have made your choices, you click on the *Next* button to move to the other sections of the Wizard. Many of

# Web site construction simplified

these are intended for much more elaborate page creation and will not be applicable to a simple home page of the type that this book is about.

The next part of the Wizard, however, is important. You are asked to fill in the page URL and Title. The URL is the filename that will appear in your Web space, and this will probably have to be *index.htm*, or whatever name is required by your IP. By contrast, the *Page Title* can be what you like, and the Wizard suggests that you use your name in this part, because this is what search engines will find. You can make this name a long one, reflecting what you want a browser to find in a search.

You will then be asked to fill in more detail about your sections. For example, if you have opted to use *Current Projects*, you will be asked to fill in names of some current projects that will appear as sub-titles in this section. The *Biographical* section will ask you if you want to use sub-headings of *Academic*, *Professional* and *Personal* (any selection or mixture of these three). For *Personal Interests*, you can fill in a list of items, and select the presentation options of bulleted list, numbered list or definition list (meaning a two-column list with each row containing an item followed by a description).

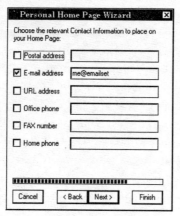

Finally, the *Contact Information* portion appears, as illustrated, allowing you to pick what details will appear so that readers can contact you.

You will then see a list of your main sections, and you can select any section by clicking on it, and then use the *Up* or *Down* buttons to alter the position of the section in the page. You can then click the *Next* button to come to the end of the Wizard, and click the *Finish* button to see the completed page. The illustration shows part of this page as it appears on the screen, before the title has been edited.

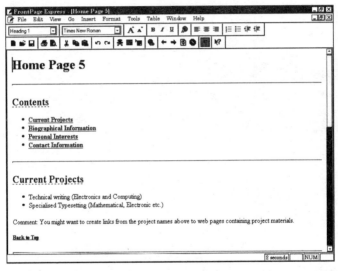

The Wizard has now created a skeleton page for you, with the advantage that the work of making internal links has been done, and if you have put your e-mail address into your contact section this also will be in hyperlink form.

At this point, you might like to take a look of the HTML codes that are used to represent this page. Click on View — HTML to see the code that will be transmitted over the net and stored in your Web site. This is displayed using NotePad, as illustrated, following.

## Web site construction simplified

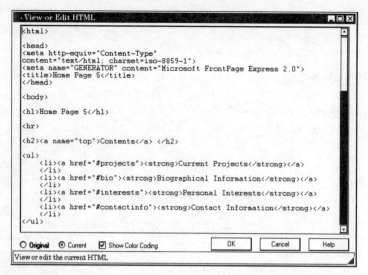

```
View or Edit HTML
<html>

<head>
<meta http-equiv="Content-Type"
content="text/html; charset=iso-8859-1">
<meta name="GENERATOR" content="Microsoft FrontPage Express 2.0">
<title>Home Page 5</title>
</head>

<body>

<h1>Home Page 5</h1>

<hr>

<h2><a name="top">Contents</a> </h2>

<ul>
    <li><a href="#projects"><strong>Current Projects</strong></a>
    </li>
    <li><a href="#bio"><strong>Biographical Information</strong></a>
    </li>
    <li><a href="#interests"><strong>Personal Interests</strong></a>
    </li>
    <li><a href="#contactinfo"><strong>Contact Information</strong></a>
    </li>
</ul>
```

O Original   ⦿ Current   ☑ Show Color Coding       OK       Cancel       Help

View or edit the current HTML

Once you have created this skeleton page, you should store it on your hard drive. Create a new folder, using a name such as Myweb, and click File — Save As. This brings up a form that is mainly intended for saving the file to the Web site, and to save to your hard drive you need first to click the *As File* button. You will then see an Explorer view so that you can browse to the folder you have created for Net pages. You can then save the page using the filename (such as *index.htm*) that has been approved by your IP.

This is important, because there is no point in saving the page as it stands to the Web. Saving to a file allows you to work on it as much as you like before anyone else sees it, and if you want to see what a browser will make of it, click on the filename (index.htm) in an Explorer view of your files and folders. This will open Internet Explorer and display the file as if it had been downloaded over the Net.

### Working with text

Once you have saved the outline of your page, you can start fleshing it out. The skills you need now are the usual word-

26

processing actions, but with a few oddities that are enforced
by the nature of HTML code.

To start with, if you have been accustomed to typing fully
justified text in your word-processor, forget it. FrontPage
Express allows you to align your text left, right or centred,
but not fully justified.

• You can format a paragraph by placing the cursor
anywhere in the paragraph and clicking one of the
alignment icons in the formatting toolbar of
FrontPage Express.

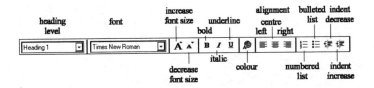

Note that if you alter the alignment of any of your
subheadings you will find the space between headings
changes. This is because the change of alignment creates a
new paragraph from text that was formerly a set of
consecutive lines, and adds new HTML code, such as:

< p align = "left" >

You can restore the spacing by clicking View — HTML and
deleting this piece of code.

• Normally, you will not have separated these sub-
headings anyhow, so that you will not be concerned by
this, but you should know what can happen if you alter
the alignment of these headings. If you press the Return
key to make a new paragraph in a bulleted list you can
remove the bullet by backspacing.

The menu route to alignment is to use the Format —
Paragraph menu and then select the option in the *Paragraph*

# Web site construction simplified

*Align* box (click the arrowhead to see the options of *Default*, *Left*, *Center* and *Right*). It is much quicker to use the icons.

Emphasis in terms of bold, italic and underlining starts by selecting the text by dragging the cursor across it. You can then click on the **B**, *I* or U̲ icon in the toolbar to carry out the action. The menu option is to use Format — Font and select from *Regular*, *Bold*, *Italic* or *Bold Italic*.

- The Format — Font menu can also be used to select the name of the font you want to use, its style (bold, etc.) size and effects (such as *Underline*, *Strikethrough* and *Typewriter*). This points out another oddity of writing for HTML code. HTML does not permit a large range of font sizes, and though you can specify a range of point sizes as 8, 10, 12, 14, 18, 24 and 36 point text, this is only an approximation.

You will find that you can change font size much more easily by using the icons that use the letter A with an arrowhead. The larger A can be clicked to increase letter size of selected text, and the smaller A can be clicked to decrease the size.

- You can indent text and alter indentation by clicking on the indent icons of FrontPage Express after placing the cursor in the indented line.

Another way of controlling your text is by selecting styles. Place the cursor in any paragraph and click the arrowhead for the *Styles* box, at the left-hand side of the formatting toolbar. This will offer a set of styles, see later, and most of your typing will use the *Normal* style because the headings, subheadings, lists, etc., have already been created by the Wizard. If, however, you are creating a page from scratch it is useful to know that you can apply these ready-made styles to get the effects you want.

| Address | Bulleted List | Defined Term |
| --- | --- | --- |
| Definition | Directory List | Formatted |
| Heading 1 | Heading 2 | Heading3 |
| Heading 4 | Heading 5 | Heading 6 |
| Menu List | Normal | Numbered List |

The template that the Wizard creates for you allows you to get to different sections on the same page (remember that a page can be as long as you like) using hyperlinks, and the template also shows how this is done. The heading *Current Projects* that lies under the index list is shown with dotted underlining, and in FrontPage Express this means that the line has been bookmarked. Bookmarking, used also in Word, inserts code so that a section of text can be identified, and using the Wizard, this is done for you. If it were not, you would have to carry out bookmarking for yourself, like this:

1. Select the word, line or phrase you want to mark.

2. Click Edit — Bookmark

3. Check the name that appears and edit it if necessary.

4. Click on OK

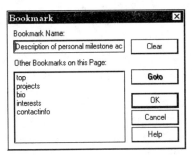

If you need references that are not provided by the Wizard, this is one half of the action. The other half is to make the hyperlink to the bookmark.

## Web site construction simplified

1.  Place the cursor where you want the link to appear and type a name so that you know what you will get when you click on that name.

2.  Select the name

3.  Click Edit — Hyperlink

4.  A form appears that  by default is at a tab called *World Wide Web*. Click on the *Open Pages* tab and then on *Home Page*. This identifies the link as being to something on this page.

5.  Now click the arrowhead on the Bookmark line, and select the bookmark name you have used for the target line. Click on the *OK* button.

This completes the action, and clicking this hyperlink will take you to the correct place on the page.

You can also create hyperlinks to other pages on your own site, or to any page on the Web. The start is always the same — you type a word, phrase or line that will be clicked to carry out the linking action, and select it. You then use the form that appears and select the tab that is appropriate. If you want to refer to a page on your own Web site, use the *Open Pages* tab and select the page.

- Note that this can be a page saved locally on your hard drive and not yet uploaded to the Web site. If you keep all of your pages in the same folder, this becomes much easier.

If you want to refer to another site, then you have to click the World Wide Web tab and then:

1. Click the arrowhead at *Hyperlink type* and select *http*.

2. Fill in the rest of the address in the *URL* line.

3. Click the *OK* button.

For a simple Web page, ignore the *Target Frame* line, which allows you to pick a particular part of the page at the URL address you have specified.

- Remember that you cannot see the results of these actions by clicking the hyperlinks as you see them in FrontPage Express. You need to look at the saved page using a browser before you can see the effects.

**Graphics**

If your page requires a graphical image, you can insert it by using the Insert menu or the *Insert Image* icon. You must first ensure that you have a suitable graphics file, meaning one that is in GIF or JPG format, and you need to know what folder contains this file.

1. Place the cursor where you want the image to appear.

2. Use Insert — Image or click the icon for the action (the postcard of mountains).

3. The panel that appears uses the *Other Location* tab and *From File* source by default, and you can click the *Browse* button.

# Web site construction simplified

4.  Click the file when you find it and then on the *Open* button. This will place the graphics picture at the cursor position.

5.  You can change the size of the picture by clicking so that the handles show and then dragging one of the corner handles — this is the method used almost universally for altering picture sizes in graphics software.

6.  You can align the picture (while the handles are showing) by using the left, centre or right alignment icons. You cannot drag a picture about the screen.

7.  If the picture covers text you will have to make a larger space for it by adding blank paragraphs.

Use graphics sparingly, because they add significantly to the downloading time. Never make a graphics item the main content of a page, but do use drawings that make text easier to understand. Be sure to have text that will indicate what the graphic displays, so that readers who have opted not to see graphics can determine whether or not to right-click and select *Show Picture*. If you use the same image several times, it need be downloaded only once.

Your page will load faster if you keep the number of graphics to a minimum and keep the size small — JPG low-resolution graphics are better viewed in small sizes. You can also assist understanding by using items such as formatting, ruled lines, tables and lists — do not rely too much on graphics. If you must have a large graphic item, put it on a separate page with a hyperlink in your index page, so that the viewer can decide whether or not to look at it.

## Tables

Tables are an important feature of Web site editors, because HTML code cannot deal with columns of text in any other way. You will find tables used extensively in Web sites that you browse over, and it's likely that you will want to use tables in your own site.

As usual, you start by placing the cursor where you want to put the table, and you can then either click the *Table* icon or use the menu item of Table — Insert Table.

1.  If you use the icon you will see a miniature table with five rows and five columns appear. Drag the cursor across this to indicate how many rows and columns you want up to a maximum of 5 × 5. If you use Table — Insert table you will see a panel that calls for you to enter the number of rows and columns, and also allows you to select width, alignment, border, cell padding and cell spacing. You will need to click the OK button when you have filled in the quantities (or use the default 2 × 2 table).

2.  If you used the icon with no width setting made, the table will appear as a miniature, but if you type text into the table the cell sizes will automatically adjust to accommodate the text. Remember that you can paste in text only from an ASCII text editor, not from Word or other formatting word processor.

## Current Projects

- Technical writing (Electronics and Computing)
- Specialised Typesetting (Mathematical, Electronic etc.

Comment: You might want to create links from the project na

Here is text

**Back to Top**

# Web site construction simplified

3.  You can paste a graphic into a cell of a table, using the same method as pasting to a paragraph. This gives you more control over where a graphic appears, and is very useful if you want to have a graphic appearing alongside text (using a two-column table).

4.  Once the table has been created, whether it contains anything or not, you can alter its features.

## Table alterations

You can insert a row or column next to a cell by first selecting the cell and then clicking Table — Insert Rows and Columns. The panel that appears allows you to select *Row* or *Column*, and the number you want to insert. If you opt for row(s) you can select above or below the cell you selected, and if you opt for column(s) you can select left or right.

You can insert a caption, in a line above the table, by placing the cursor in any cell and using Table — Select Table, then Table — Insert caption.

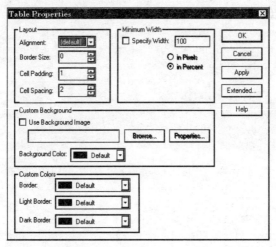

Other table alterations are done using *Table Properties* as illustrated here. You can reach this panel either by right-clicking on any cell and clicking *Table Properties*, or by clicking the menu item Table — Table Properties.

You can now alter the features of the complete table as follows. Note that the panel contains an *Apply* button that you can click to see the effect of your choices before you click the *OK* button to fix the change. If you do not like the effect you see when you click *Apply*, you can opt for the *Cancel* button.

**Layout**. This is divided into *Alignment*, *Border size*, *Cell padding* and *Cell spacing*. The *Alignment* is selected as *Left*, *Center* or *Right* and it will affect the position of any table that is less wide than the page. *Border size* affects the outside border around the whole table, and *Cell spacing* affects the border area round each cell. *Cell padding* places spacing between the cell contents (text or graphics) and the cell border.

- The Cell spacing and padding options can be used to create interesting 3D effects when a border is also used. The illustration shows the effects of Border=2, Cell padding=4 and Cell spacing=5 on a small table.

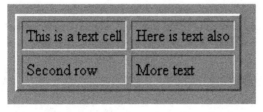

**Minimum width**. This part of the Table Properties allows you to specify the minimum width of the whole table. If you opt to use this (by ticking the box) you can use the percentage option, initially set to 100% of page width, or the pixel option (100 pixels default). The percentage option is often more useful.

**Custom Background**. You can use this if you want to make use of either a picture or solid colour as a background for the

# Web site construction simplified

whole table. If you opt for a picture (which must be in GIF or JPG format) remember that a detailed picture will make it difficult to see anything in your table, unless you have a picture that has been created in or converted to pale transparent colours. When you opt for a picture you will see the *Insert Picture* panel, offering *Clipart* or *Other Location*, and you can browse for a suitable image.

- A large image will appear as a background to the entire table, but a small image is likely to appear as a repeated background for each cell. Use the *Apply* button to check on what will appear.

- Any graphics file used in this way will have to be copied to the Web site eventually, so you should make a copy in your Web folder on the hard drive once you have decided to use the file. You will then have to alter the *Properties* panel to show the new site of the file and since it exists in the same folder you need only use the filename. To be more correct, you can prefix the filename with .\ (dot backslash) to indicate that it is in the same folder.

If you clear the box that allows a picture background, you can use colour background. Click on the arrowhead next to the *Background Color* line in *Table Properties*, and select the colour you want to use. Once again, you have to be careful that your choice does not make the table difficult to read.

- You need to click the *OK* button to see the effect of your choice of picture or colour background appear on the table.

- The boxes marked *Transparent* and *Interlaced* will appear ticked or cleared according to the properties of the image that you insert. Changing these does not appear to make much difference. For a JPG image you can select *Resolution* so as to match your screen resolution.

The last portion of the *Table Properties* panel allows choice of border colours. You can opt for a *Border* colour that will affect the whole table (dark for the outside table border and paler between cells), or you can opt for separate light and dark borders that give a 3D effect.

**Cell properties**

The Table properties affect the whole table, no matter what cell contains the cursor. There is another panel for Cell properties, affecting only the cell that contains the cursor. This panel contains more options than the Table properties panel. It also contains the *Apply* button so that you can see the effects of a change before fixing it.

- You can, however, use *Select Row* or *Select Column* from the Table menu so that your Cell properties affect all of the cells in a selected row or column. If you use *Select Table* then all the cells of the table will be affected by any changes you make in the cell properties.

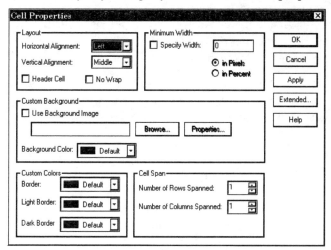

## Web site construction simplified

**Layout**. This affects the positioning of the contents of the cell. You can select *Horizontal alignment* as *Left*, *Center* or *Right*, and *Vertical alignment* as *Top*, *Middle* or *Bottom* of the cell. The selection box items are *Header cell* and *No wrap*. Click *Header cell* if this is a cell that carries a heading for the column — the text will then appear in bold. The *No wrap* box seems to have no visible effect, and when it has been ticked you need to click on it twice to make the tick disappear completely — the first click greys the tick.

**Minimum width**. You can specify that your selected cell will have a minimum width. The effects of this are not necessarily straightforward, because only the selected cell is affected, not a complete column, unless you have selected a complete column. For example, if you have a cell containing three words with a 20-word cell under it, selecting the 3-word cell and reducing its width can make the words appear in three separate lines, but the cell boundary will still be the same as that of the other cells in the column. The boundaries change only if you have selected the column.

**Custom background.** You can use this section to display either a picture or a colour as a background to your selected cell. The action is exactly the same as that in *Table Properties*, and any picture file should be put into the folder that contains all Web site material.

**Custom Colors**. This acts in exactly the same way as the corresponding options in *Table Properties*, but affects only the selected cell(s).

**Cell span**. This option allows you to expand a cell by taking in the next cell to the right (column span) or underneath (row span). This does not work like cell merging in Word, and the number of columns or rows may be increased rather then decreased by this action. Always use the *Apply* button before you click the *OK* button after using this action.

## Other formatting

Bulleted and numbered lists will have been put into your page if you opted to use the Wizard, but you might want more lists. With the cursor placed where you want to use a list, click the Format — Bullets and Numbering menu item. Select which of these you want, and choose from the styles that are available. You can select from three types of bullets and five types of numbering, with a final choice of neither.

If you see the *Other* tab appear, it can be used if you want to pick the type of list you want to create, with a choice of *Bulleted list, Definition list, Directory list, Menu list,* or *Numbered list.* There is a box marked *Compact Layout* that can be used for a *Definition* list, and which will make the list tidier when the individual items are short.

- When you have created a line with bulleting or numbering, typing text into this line and then pressing the Return key will create another bulleted or numbered line — press Return again without typing anything if you want to end the effect.

- You can remove any formatting effects from selected text by using Format — Remove formatting.

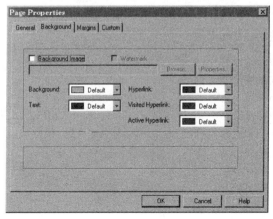

# Web site construction simplified

The *Background* for your entire page can be controlled by using Format — Background. This leads to a tab which is also reached by right-clicking on your page and selecting *Page Properties*, then *Background*. You can reach this also from File — Page Properties.

Like the table background, this panel allows you to use either a background picture or a colour. If you use a picture you will have to edit it to ensure that it uses light transparent colours that will not obscure your page. Though a selection box is marked *Watermark*, ticking this does not make the image transparent, and clicking the *Properties* button to find the *Transparent* selection box does not help.

• Remember that the picture file should be placed in the same folder as your HTM page file, and that the Properties should show the filename without any path, or with the .\ path only.

As an alternative, you can use the *Background* colour selector — even this can result in backgrounds that are too strong to allow some details to be clearly seen. The other colour options in this set allow you to set colours for text, hyperlink, active hyperlink, and visited hyperlink. These are best left at their defaults unless you have some special need to change them.

## Other page properties

The *General* tab for *Page Properties*, visible when you right-click on the page and then on *Page Properties*, contains a list of titles, *Location* (which is the local hard drive file location), *Title*, *Base Location* and *Default Target Frame*. These last two will be blank if your page is still being constructed and exists only on the hard drive, and will appear only if you have opened the page from its Web site.

Another section on this tab allows you to have background sound, and allows you to browse for a suitable sound file.

For a short sound clip you can opt for a number of repeats or for the sound clip to repeat for as long as the page is being viewed. As for graphics, the sound file will eventually have to be placed on your Web site, so that you should copy or move it to the hard drive folder that contains your other Web site files.

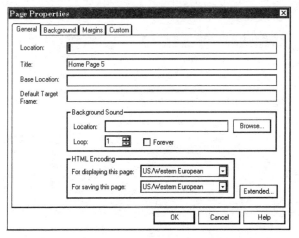

The portion of this tab that deals with HTML coding will be set to *US/Western European* by default, and no change is needed unless you want to construct a site using another family of languages.

The *Margins* tab allows you to opt for left and top margins for your page and to specify them as a number of pixels. Use this only if your page seems to be set too far over to the left or top when viewed in a browser.

**Other inserts**

Insert — Break allows you to break a line. This is not the same as using the Return key to make a new paragraph, because the break is a line break (also called a Newline break), with a smaller spacing between the lines than you get using a new paragraph. As well as the normal line break you can opt for *Clear Left Margin*, *Clear Right Margin* and

## Web site construction simplified

*Clear Both Margins* if you prefer the appearance of one of these options.

Insert — Horizontal line will place a full-width horizontal line at the cursor position. This line is by default a pair of thin lines separated by two pixels and not filled, and you can alter the appearance by right-clicking on the line and then on *Horizontal Line Properties*.

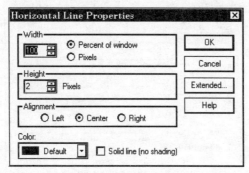

You can then alter the *Width*, either in terms of percentage of page width (default 100%) or in terms of screen pixels. The line *Height* (its thickness) is set at 2 pixels, but you can adjust this as you wish — a 1 pixel line is the thinnest you can achieve. The alignment can be selected as left, centred or right. The last adjustment is *Color*. If the *Solid line* box is left blank, the default line will appear with a colour on top and white below. You can alter this either by specifying a solid line or by selecting a colour from the list that appears when the arrowhead is clicked.

Insert — Symbol is used when you want to place into your text some character that cannot be obtained using the keyboard, such as accented foreign characters or marks such as ©,®, € (the Euro currency sign) or ™. When you select a symbol insert, you will see the list appear. Clicking on an item will display an enlarged version in the box next to the *Insert* button. You can then click the *Insert* button to place the symbol at the cursor position, and then the *Close* button to return to normal typing. You can insert more than one symbol before using the *Close* key.

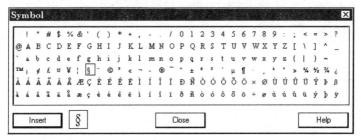

- Note that the € symbol will appear only if you have it installed in your font. It is often easier to read text containing this symbol from a Word file, because it is easier to control which font is used in Word.

Insert — Comment allows you to put comments into your page that will not appear when the page is browsed from the Web site. You might use a comment to remind yourself that some item will need to be updated, or why you have used a graphic. When you insert a comment, a panel will appear. Note that FrontPage Express shows a robot icon (the *WebBot*) when the cursor is over a comment, because this is an action that can be provided as a *WebBot*. Some Web sites may not accept such items, so you should not use comments unless your IP indicates that they will work as you expect them to.

Of the other *Insert* items, some such as *Image* are more easily done using icons, others are not easy for the beginner to use. You should not incorporate a video clip into your index page because it downloads too slowly, and if you must include such material you should put it on a separate page so that the viewer has the option. *WebBot Components* should be avoided unless you are certain that your IP permits them, and the *Other Components* section is for programs in languages such as Java, a definite no-no for beginners (and for most of the rest of us also). *Form Fields* should also be

43

avoided until you have considerable experience with Web design — they allow you to create fill-in forms that a viewer can complete, with the results being fed back to you. *Script* is another type of insert that requires programming experience.

*Scrolling Marquee* allows you to have text that scrolls or oscillates across the screen, like the Windows screensaver of the same name. This effect seems to work on most Web sites, and when you click this menu item you will see a *Marquee Properties* panel appear.

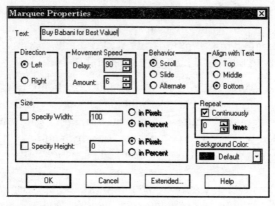

The *Text* box of this panel is initially blank, allowing you to type in whatever slogan or other text you want. Remember to take care over this text because unless you paste it in using the Ctrl-V key combination there is no way of spell-checking it. Remember that pasting must be from an ASCII text editor, so that an ideal candidate is CNotePad, which supports spell-checking.

• Checking the result of inserting a *Marquee* is difficult because no movement appears until the HTML file is browsed. Fortunately this can be done by clicking on the *index.htm* file in your hard drive folder, and you do not have to upload to the Web first.

You can then select the direction left or right, and the movement speed in terms of delay (time between each movement) and amount (number pixels moved).

You can select the behaviour of your *Marquee* as *Scroll*, *Slide* or *Alternate*. You will find that there is little difference between the appearance of *Scroll* and *Slide* with the default speed settings, but *Alternate* causes a noticeable to and fro action. The *Align with Text* options of *Top*, *Middle* and *Bottom* will also not be apparent unless the *Marquee* is separated from the nearest text.

You can alter the size of the *Marquee* text by using the *Height* portion of the *Size* selection, and you can also change the width of the scrolling part by specifying either the percentage or pixel width. Normally, you will make a *Marquee* extend over 100% of the page width.

The only other options are for number of repetitions (or continuous repetition), and the colour of the text. You can alter your *Marquee* specification at any time while you have your page loaded into FrontPage Express, by right-clicking on the *Marquee* space and selecting **Marquee Properties**.

The only remaining Insert item is *Hyperlink*, which has been dealt with earlier on page 29.

## Using Word

Microsoft Word is a vast word processing package with a range of actions that few users ever explore exhaustively, and if you have the most recent version, Word 97 (or Word-8.0) then you can use it to create Web pages and save them in HTM format. Since readers who have not installed Windows 98 or Explorer 4.0 will not have FrontPage Express, a brief description of Word's capabilities might be useful.

To start with, using Word avoids any need to learn HTML coding, because you can use Word normally and then save your file in HTM format, using the File — Save As menu. The editing is close to WYSIWYG, but you need to watch some items that can be placed into a Word document but which do **not** convert correctly into HTML.

You can construct your Web pages using wizards and templates that are part of Word. This assumes that you installed *Web Authoring* as part of your Word installation. If you did not, it should be possible to install this option later, but in some cases it is not possible, and no fix for this is known to date. You can, however, create pages using Word in the normal way and save the resulting file as HTML without using the *Web Authoring Wizard*.

You can use drag and drop for Web page elements, and you have access to all the actions of Word such as background colours, bullets, horizontal lines, spell checking, AutoText, AutoCorrect, grammar checking, tables, drawing objects and WordArt.

What you have to be careful about is the list of items that Word can place into a document but which cannot be converted into HTML format. These include fields, such as the automatic insertion of a date into a document. In addition, you have to know how some Word features convert.

**Borders**: HTML does not support the use of page borders and borders around paragraphs and words. If you have used these, they will be removed, though borders around your tables will remain unchanged.

**Bullets and Numbering**: The bullets that you use in Word are converted to filled-in circles. Numbered lists will convert, but you should not use the option of numbers between brackets. The HTML version will use ½" hanging indents.

- Once a document has been converted to HTML format, you can read it back and use Format — Bullets and

Numbering to choose graphical bullets rather than the bullets used in normal Word documents.

**Comments:** If you have placed comments in a Word document, these will be deleted upon conversion to HTML. You can, however, reload the HTML file and then type comments.

**Pictures:** Drawings that you create in a Word document by using the tools on the Drawing toolbar disappear when the document is converted to HTML. This includes items such as AutoShapes, text boxes, and shadows. You can re-create these items when you reload the HTML file using Insert — Object, and selecting Microsoft Word Picture. This will open a panel so that you can use the drawing tools to create a picture. The next time you close the document, the drawing will be converted to a GIF image.

**Drop Caps:** If you have used drop caps in a document, they will be removed when you save in HTML format. On an HTML document, however, you can select a single character and use the *Increase Font Size* button. Another method that you will see used is to insert a graphics image of a large capital letter.

**Equations and charts**: All of these items are converted to GIF images when you save in HTML format. Remember that you must store the GIF images in your Web folder or in a form that is accessible. You cannot edit these items once they are converted, so you should keep a copy of the original document in which they appear.

**Fields:** Field codes that are used in Word, such as current date, are removed, but the value of each field will be saved as text. This value cannot be automatically updated.

**Fonts**: Fonts used in a Word document are converted to the nearest available HTML size. The HTML font sizes are expressed as numbers in the range 1–7, which correspond roughly to point sizes in the range 9–36. If you use animated fonts, the animation disappears, and only the value at the time of saving the file is retained.

**Effects:** The normal font effects of bold italic and underline are unchanged, but dotted underlines will be converted to solid. Fancy effects such as embossed, shadow, engraved, small caps, all caps, strikethrough, and outline are all lost when the text is converted to HTML.

**Headers, footers, footnotes, endnotes**: These are not permitted in HTML, so all will disappear. Page numbering also disappears because each HTML file is a single page.

**Highlighting**: Highlighting is not supported in HTML.

**Index, table of contents:** These tables are converted to text, so that they will no longer be updated automatically if the pagination changes.

**Margins:** These are removed on conversion to HTML. If you need to control page layout, use tables.

**Newspaper columns:** These also are removed. If you need columns, you have to make use of tables.

**Revision marks:** You would normally have completed revision of a document by the time you converted it to HTML. Any changes that have been confirmed will be retained but the revision marks for other changes are not.

**Styles:** If you have defined styles for yourself and used them in a document they will be converted to the nearest format that is supported in HTML.

**Tables:** Word tables will be converted, using a fixed width.

**Tabs:** Word tabs are converted to HTML characters which will appear simply as spaces in some browsers. You should use indents and tables for preference.

**Text boxes:** These and the text they contain will disappear when the file is saved as HTML.

### Word Tables

Though Word can create impressive tables, you will find that they do not appear so satisfactory when converted to HTML and viewed by a browser. These notes will help in creating tables that will survive conversion and still be recognisable.

The Insert — Table command of Word, or the icon for table creation, will create a table that is, at most, 5 columns by 4 rows, and the columns are equally spaced. The snag is that the default width of a Word table is more than your browser is likely to be able to display. Reduce the width of a Word table before you save the document, select the table, and use Table — Distribute Columns Evenly.

You would normally extend a Word table by moving the cursor just to the right of the last cell in the table and pressing the Return key to add another row. For a document that is to be saved in HTML format you should use the longer method, Table — Insert Row. You should also avoid using the Word action of splitting a row.

If you want to alter the width of a column in a Word table, either drag the dividing line between columns, or the button that appears in the Ruler line when a table is selected. You will need to adjust overall width to make certain that none of the table moves outside the width that the browser can cope with.

Adding a column presents problems, because though Word can deal with an extra column by adjusting other columns,

# Web site construction simplified

this adjustment does not appear when the document is converted to HTML and viewed by a browser. The recommended method is to select a column and use Table — Split cells. Enter the number of new columns and click on the OK button.

Now select all columns and use Table — Distribute Columns Evenly if you want columns of equal width.

## Word graphics

Word has particularly good graphics handling, assuming that you installed all of the graphics filters when you installed Word. For Web pages, the GIF and JPG file types are the most common, but you can also insert graphics files as bitmaps (BMP), metafiles (WMF), and many others, including Corel Draw! files and the DXF files used by CAD programs.

There are two different methods that you can use to insert a graphics file into a Word document. If you use Insert — Picture — From File this allows you to browse for graphics files from your hard drive, a floppy or from the Web. Alternatively, you can make use of the huge store of Clipart images that come with Word by using Insert — Picture — Clipart. You are reminded when you use this option that you can insert the Word CD-ROM to obtain a much larger selection of Clipart.

## Link insertion

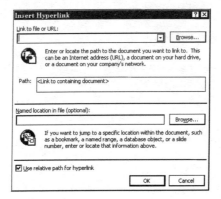

Word can use its Insert menu to deal with your hyperlinks, and you can link to another file, another Web site or to a bookmarked piece of text in the same document. When you click on Insert — Hyperlink you will see the panel appear. You need to fill in the upper portion for another document or a Web site, or the lower portion if you want to jump to a bookmark that you have made earlier using Insert — Bookmark.

## AOLpress

AOLpress is a WYSIWYG editor combined with a net browser, and in this respect it resembles Amaya (see page 64). AOLpress is free to non-commercial users, and is packaged along with the AOL (America OnLine) net connection software. It can be downloaded from the site *davecentral.com*. AOLpress is not too complex for beginners, and is also a useful editor for the more experienced user, particularly anyone using AOL as an Internet provider. You will need at least 8 Mbyte of hard drive space free to install AOLpress.

AOLpress is distributed in the form of a file called aolp20_32.exe. This is a compressed file that can be run so as to extract all the components of AOLpress to a temporary

## Web site construction simplified

folder, from which you can then run its Setup.exe program to install the main program files. You will be asked to select a folder for installation, a Start menu entry, and if you want an icon placed on the Desktop.

- When you have installed AOLpress, print out the README.TXT file for information on known bugs and methods of overcoming problems. Many of these points will be of concern only to the more advanced user.

### Starting work

When AOLpress starts it shows an introductory screen that can be removed by clicking its OK button, and another screen, illustrated here, that can be removed by using File — Close. To remove this screen permanently, use Tools — Preferences — General — Startup View and remove the dot that selects *Home Page*.

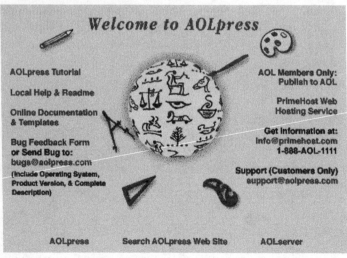

This then leaves you with an uncluttered screen that contains only the menu line of File, Tools, Browse, Windows and Help. One of the attractions of using AOLpress is that it is a browser also, so that once you have set it up you can click the Browse menu item and look at your favourite sites. You can also use this action to examine any HTM files you have created so that you can check how they display.

To display any HTM file that is stored on your hard drive, click File — Open and in the *Location* line type the filename and path (such as C:\data\myweb\index.htm). Alternatively, you can use the *Directory list* to browse for files. This list uses the convention of two dots to mean the next higher folder, so that if you double-click on the dots you can move one folder up in the view. If you are uncertain, you can make navigation easier by using the *All Files* option of *Files of Type*.

- You normally see your file in WYSIWYG form, as a browser would see it. If you want to see the HTML code, click Tools — Show HTML. This opens a new window, and you can use the Window menu to return to the normal text display.

URLs for pages on the Web can be used in the *Location* line also. The problem here is that if you normally use Microsoft Internet Explorer, you cannot see your Explorer's History list in AOLpress. You can, however, transfer a site URL as follows:

1. Start AOLpress and use File — Open. Delete any URL that appears in the Location line.

2. Use Explorer to find your Windows *History* or *Favorites* folder, and right-click on any URL you want to use.

3. Select *Copy*, switch back to AOLpress and place the cursor in the *Location* line.

4. Press Ctrl–V to paste the URL into AOLpress, and you can then click *Open* to make the contact.

- If you have cancelled a connection, perhaps you did not want to continue with it, you may find that AOLpress

# Web site construction simplified

will not make any other connections until you restart the program.

- If you make any connection using AOLpress you can copy it to the HotPage, which is the AOLpress equivalent of Explorer's Favorites list.

- If a URL contains links you can follow a link by clicking on it in the normal way.

**Starting your own page**

FrontPage Express uses Wizards to generate outline pages, but this method is not a feature of most other page creating editors. You start creating a page in AOLpress by using File — New and selecting *New Page*. The blank page will appear with a reminder on the *Title* line that you should type your own title. Do this by deleting the title in the line under the Location line, and typing your new title. This will appear in the shaded text window when you move the cursor back into that window.

You can then cut/copy and paste text from any text editor or from a word processor, including Word. AOLpress will accept text from Word just as if it were ordinary ASCII text, but without any formatting — you have to do your formatting in AOLpress.

• Note that the AOLpress icons allow only left or centred text, but you can use the menu Format — Paragraph to obtain right aligned and fully aligned (left and right) text, a facility that is lacking in FrontPage Express.

You can, obviously, also type your own text, and the illustration shows some of the icons of AOLpress that you can use to format the text as you create it. One considerable advantage of using AOLpress is that it contains a spelling checker (click on the icon that shows ABC with a tick), and this is very useful if you do not have a word processor or a text editor with spelling correction. The illustration omits the first four icons of *Cut*, *Copy*, *Paste* and *Copy URL*.

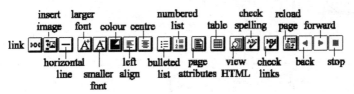

The text editing actions that you can apply by clicking icons include the usual cut, copy and paste, with horizontal bar, font size and colour, and alignment. These work very much in the same way as the corresponding icons of FrontPage Express operate. These facilities allow you to build up a page with index items, headings and sub-headings, bars and other effects.

• You can also bring text into your page from other files by choosing File — Import.

# Web site construction simplified

## Page colours and backgrounds

AOLPress allows you to use either a colour or a background image for your pages. Start this action from Format — Page Attributes. The panel that appears has a large number of controls, starting with *Colour* and *Background Picture*. You can use a *Pick* button to select a *Background Color*, or the *Browse* button for a picture. There is also a useful option to import the background picture file into the same folder as your HTML files.

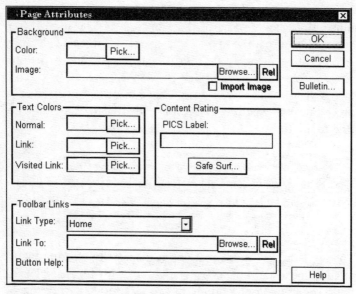

The text colours can also be altered, and because AOLpress is a browser you can specify content ratings to be used to prevent the more objectionable type of material from being downloaded.

The *Bulletin* button allows you to add a hidden comment along with time and date. The *Toolbar Links* section allows you to place tool icons that will affect your Web page. These icons appear in the browser if your browser supports this action — and Internet Explorer 4.0 does not. If you intend to use AOLpress as your main or only browser, however, you can select one or more links to the following:

|           |                   |           |
|-----------|-------------------|-----------|
| Home      | Table of Contents | Index     |
| Glossary  | Copyright         | Up        |
| Next      | Previous          | Help      |
| Backward  | First page        | Last page |

**Links**

Links are also created in much the same way as in FrontPage Express, except that you have to learn new names. In place of a *Bookmark* we have an *Anchor*, so that when you select a subheading that you want to link to you need to use the Element — Anchor menu item, and specify a name if the default (usually the first word of the selected phrase) is not suitable. You can then click the *OK* button to establish this marker. At the index line, or wherever the link is to start, select again and use Element — Link. You will have to type the anchor name into the *Append Anchor Name* line because no list of names will be shown. This makes the process just a bit more difficult than the corresponding FrontPage Express system.

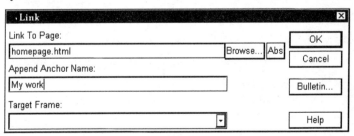

If you need a link to a Web site, then type or paste the URL into the *Link to Page* line of the Link panel.

You can make use of preformatted headings as follows:

## Web site construction simplified

1. Put your text cursor in a line that you want to use as a heading.

2. Click Format — Heading and select from Hdg1 (largest) to Hdg6 (smallest). Alternatively you can use keys Ctrl–1 to Ctrl–6.

3. You can remove a heading by using Format — Remove Heading Format.

### Styles

Like any word processor, AOLpress makes use of styles that apply to a selected paragraph, with each use of the Enter/Return key creating a new paragraph. When you click Format — Paragraph you will find three style options of *BlockQuote*, *Preformatted* and *Address*. The *BlockQuote* option will indent your paragraph from each side, the *Preformatted* option will convert to a monospaced font (like a typewriter) all in one line, and the *Address* style will convert the text to indented italics.

When you press Return at the end of such a paragraph, the cursor will move down and left ready to make another paragraph of the same style. You can prevent this by using Format — Exit Paragraph Format so that the cursor moves to the next line allowing you to type a normal paragraph.

• You can use Format — Remove Paragraph Format to remove all formatting you have applied from the paragraph that contains the cursor.

You do not need to use paragraphs simply in order to take a new line. If you use Shift–Return in place of the Return key used by itself, the line is broken with a single space between lines. Any style that you apply will affect all these lines up to the point where you used the Return key to end a paragraph. Another line break option is the menu item of Element — Forced Line Break.

## Character styles

Character styles apply to selected characters, which could be anything from one character to one line or more of text. The styles have to be selected from a menu — there are no buttons for the usual bold, italic and underline set. As compensation, AOLpress offers a large set of styles, consisting of *bold*, *italic*, *underline*, *fixed-pitch*, *deleted*, *new*, *subscript*, *superscript*, *citation*, *code*, *definition*, *emphasis*, *keyboard*, *sample*, *strong*, and *variable*. These are all obtained from the Format — Typestyle menu, and can be applied to any text that you have selected.

You can apply more than one style, as many as you want to click, but you have to use the menu all over again for each style you add. There is no option to tick more than one style at a time. If you select a style before typing, your typing will then be in that style. You can return to normal text by using Format — Type Style — Plain.

- For your own pages, it's best to stick to bold, italic and underline if you need them, because you cannot be sure how the other styles will look when viewed by other browsers.

You can change the colour of text by selecting it and clicking the *Custom Color* icon, or using the Format — Type Color menu. Coloured text should be used vary sparingly, and you should avoid using colours that could make your text look like a hyperlink.

## List and table options

The list options of AOLpress are *Bulleted lists*, *Numbered lists*, and *Definition Lists*.

You can start any of these lists by clicking the Format — List menu, but for the more common bulleted and numbered type you can click the icons that appear in the Toolbar of AOLpress. If you use the menu to select a definition list, the

# Web site construction simplified

first word or phrase is referred to as the item and the second is the definition. The definition is placed on the line below the item and indented. If you place the cursor on any portion of a definition list, the Format — List menu will indicate with a tick whether this is an item or a definition, and you can use this also to place more than one definition for an item, or to create an item with no definition.

Once you have started a list, each use of the Return key will create a new list item. You can use Format — Exit List Format to return to normal, and if you have made a nested list (a list within a list) you will have to use this action more than once. You can also use Format — Remove List Format to convert a list into normal text.

A table is started by clicking the Table icon or the menu item of Table — Create Table. Either way, you will see the Table panel appearing.

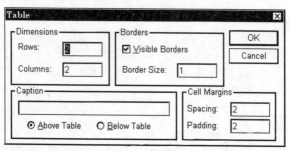

You can then fill in the quantities that you want, or accept the defaults. The *Dimensions* set is used for the number of rows and columns, and the default is 2 for each. The *Border* set has *Visible Borders* option ticked by default, with a size of 1 pixel. The *Caption* space allows you to type text to use as a caption and you can opt for this to be placed above or below the table. Finally, the *Cell Margins* are set in terms of *Cell Spacing* and *Cell Padding*, with a default of 2 pixels for each.

- If you need to type text into table cells, you may find that your typing speed is restricted unless you are using a fast computer. This is because the table is constantly being resized as you type.

You can escape from a table (if your cursor is in the table) by using Format — Exit Table, or you can delete a table by placing the cursor in the table and clicking Format — Remove Table format.

- Once the skeleton table appears you can place the cursor into any cell and type or paste text, or paste images, create a list or even insert another table.

When you have created a table, you can place the cursor into a cell and use Table — Alter to create a new row, delete a row, insert a new column, delete a column, or use the *Alter* option to specify a different set of properties. A new row will be inserted above the row that contains the cursor, and a new column will be inserted to the left of the column that contains the cursor. When you use the delete options, the row or column that contains the cell with the cursor is deleted, but you will be prompted to confirm if the cells are not empty.

You can merge cells using Table — Merge Cell so that two or more cells become a single cell of the combined width or depth. The panel that appears for a merge allows you to select how many columns and rows will be used, with the default of two columns, 1 row. The merging will affect cells to the right (for merged columns) and below (for rows), but no new cells will be created. You can also split a cell that was created by merging cells (using Table — Split Cell), but you cannot split a cell that was **not** previously merged.

- Cell merging affects the cell contents. After a merge, only the content of the cell that was in the top-left position will survive. If you need items that were in the other cells, make copies by selecting each item in turn and using Copy and Paste.

- You can select a table for copying if you start your selection at the paragraph above the table and end it at the paragraph below. You cannot select a table by itself.

When you make use of a cell, any text that you type will be left-aligned by default, and other items inserted by pasting will also be left aligned. The vertical alignment is central. You can alter these alignments by using the text alignment icons (or Format — Paragraph) for horizontal alignment, and Table menu items of *V Align* for vertical alignment. If you want to alter the vertical alignment of a complete row, you can use the Table — V Align Row in place of V Align Cell.

- You can also designate cells as header cells, used for titles and (by default) in bold type. Use Table — Header Cell with the cursor in the cell you want to change.

**Pictures**

Images can be added to an AOLpress page as easily as to a word-processor document. As for all Web pages, you need to ensure that your images are in GIF or JPG format.

1. Place the cursor where you want the image to appear.

2. Click the *Image Insert* icon, or use the Element — Image menu. You will see a panel appear.

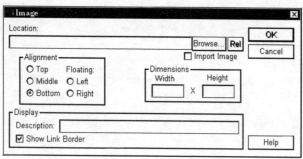

3. Type a file name and path in the *Location* space, or click the *Browse* button to find a folder that contains files. Select a file.

4. Click *OK* to insert the image at the cursor position.

There are a few useful extra facilities. If the file is in a folder that is not part of the AOLpress set, you can click the box marked *Import Image* to copy it to the AOLpress folder. If the *Abs* button appears next to the *Browse* button, you can click this to ensure that the absolute Web address of the image will be stored in your Web page. If the button appears as *Rel*, then only the relative address (relative to the folder you are using for HTML files) will appear. See page 74 for more details of absolute and relative addressing.

You can also insert images by using Copy and Paste methods, either from images that you view in a paint program, or images that you have downloaded from the Web. Note that if you publish any image (and that includes putting it into your own Web page) you will need to check that no copyright is being violated.

**Image manipulation**

When you import an image, it is placed by default at the cursor position, left aligned, and at the size of the original file copy. You may need to re-position the picture and change its size.

1. Double-click on the image. You will see *handles* appear to show that the image is now selected.

2. Drag a handle to change the image size. For most purposes, it's better to hold down the Shift key and drag a corner handle, so ensuring that the ratio of height to width of the picture is unchanged.

# Web site construction simplified

- Image width and height information is stored in the HTML code. This allows space to be allocated to the image before it downloads.

- If you want to return to the original size, select the image and right-click it (or click Element — Image). Delete the numbers that appear in the *Width* and *Height* boxes and then click the OK button.

You can alter the alignment of your image also from the panel that appears when you select and right-click. The image will always be aligned so that it does not cover text around it, and you can choose from *Top*, *Middle* or *Bottom*, and from the floating options of *Left* or *Right*.

## Amaya

Amaya is another fully-featured WYSIWYG editor that can be downloaded from a number of sites — try a search on the words Amaya or Thot. It originates in the World Wide Web Consortium, and is freeware, provided that it is used only for your own non-commercial purposes and is not modified in any way. The full legal copyright position is detailed in a document that accompanies the program. An on-line manual can be downloaded.

- Amaya is not intended for beginners, and it is strongly biased to academic users, but a brief description will illustrate how much is available when you have some experience with Web site editing.

Like AOLpress, a feature of Amaya is that it can act both as a method of writing Web pages, and also as a browser for the Web. It is also one of the very few programs available as freeware that allows mathematical work to be written in HTML form — a Word equation is by contrast, converted to a GIF file before being saved. A spell-checker is provided and also the familiar word-processor action of *Search and Replace*.

When you have installed Amaya it will be placed in a THOT folder within your Program Files folder, and a shortcut will be put into the Start menu. Clicking this shortcut will start Amaya with a *Welcome* page, and using File — New will start another copy with a blank page that you can convert into your Web page. There are no Wizards to assist you.

**Browsing**

Amaya behaves like AOLpress as far as browsing is concerned. To browse the Web, you type a URL into the *Address* line and press the Return key. There is no provision for a *Favorites* list or a *History* list, so that the browsing action of Amaya is best reserved for examining the HTML files it has created on your hard drive.

- Any links that exist in a Web document you are browsing are displayed in blue, and you must **double**-click a link to activate it — a single-click is an editing action that positions the cursor.

If you browse while you are editing a document you will be prompted to save your own document, because a downloaded page will replace your document. The alternative action is to create a new window for the Web document.

- If you want to see the HTML code for a page, click View — Show Structure. The page that appears does not resemble the HTML view that you will get with other editors, because it shows the extent of a command by using graphics lines rather than the <begin> and <end> type of codes that are present in the HTML text. This does, however, make checking easier.

- The illustration, following, has been processed to remove the annoying dotted background that appears on the Amaya HTML display and on its New Page display.

# Web site construction simplified

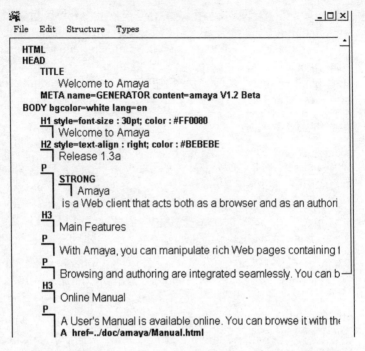

- Two points about the current version of Amaya need to be appreciated. One is that selection by dragging the mouse is often very hesitant, and it is difficult to ensure that you have selected what you want. Patience is needed. The other point is that the **right-hand** mouse button is ignored, so that you have to look for menu methods for actions that you might expect to be carried out with a right-hand button click.

## Text

You start creating a page by selecting File — New. Text can be typed or it can be pasted in from any editor or word processor. If you use text copied from a word processor document, all formatting will be lost.

The illustration has, as before, been edited to remove the dotted background.

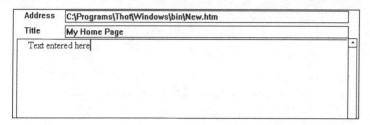

During text entry you can use the icons on the toolbar to configure your text. The icons for character formatting actions are italic (called *emphasis*), bold (called *strong*) and monospaced (*fixed font*, with a TT icon). These three are followed by *Insert Image*, and three levels of heading styles. The list icons allow for bulleted, number and definition lists. The final three icons are labelled *Link*, *Table* and *Maths*.

- You can insert and change characters by using the *Types* menu. Among many others, it allows for six levels of headings.

The Style — Character style allows you to select a style for a selected character or set of characters, using a large range of options, illustrated.

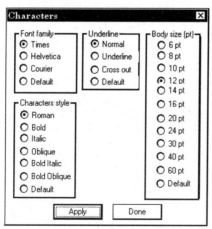

The Style — Colors menu allows you to pick foreground and background colours for the selected part of your page.

## Web site construction simplified

This has to be used with some care in case you make text unreadable, and you should save your page before you make this type of change.

You can use Style — Format to display a panel titled *Dialog* which allows you to pick alignment options of left, right, centre or default. You can also use options for *Indent*, *Justification* and *Line spacing* from this menu.

*Alignment* can be *left*, *central* or *right* and you can use the *Justification* options of *Yes*, *No* or *Default*. You may need to try out a few options before you find the settings that produce what you want. The option for setting line spacing is unusual in Editors.

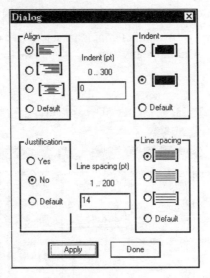

- If you want to add a horizontal line, use Types — Horizontal rule.

A table is much more difficult to achieve in Amaya than in other editors. Clicking the Table icon will create only a single cell, because Amaya does **not** use a table editor as such. You use the icon to create a single-cell, and then type or paste in what you want it to contain. Pressing the Return key twice will then create another cell in the same row, and you can then enter text or other data in that one. When you come to the last cell in a row, pressing the Return key three times will create a new row with the same number of cells as the first, and so on.

- Note that if you press Return when a cell is empty, this will simply move the cursor down a line.

- When you remove text or other content from a cell, the cell becomes redundant, and if a row or column becomes empty it will simple disappear.

**Pictures**

To insert a picture at the cursor position, click the icons or use Types — Image. The *Open location* panel will appear, requiring you to type a URL for a Web page, or to click the *Browse* button to find a local file. You will be shown the file pathname and asked to confirm. The picture is inserted when you click the *Confirm* button. As always, the picture type should be GIF or JPG, though PNG and BMP types can be used.

# Web site construction simplified

## Links

Amaya uses the Links menu or button to create and remove hyperlinks. For a link to text on the same page you must first create a target anchor. Select the text you want to find by clicking a link, and use Links — Create Target. With the usual default settings, you will see an icon appear at the start of the target text (an archery target). Click Views — Show Targets if you do not see this icon clearly. Amaya will create a reference name automatically for each target

Now move to the word, phrase or image that you want to use as a hyperlink. Select it, and click the *Links* icon or use Links — Create link. A pointing hand icon will appear, and you need to point this to the target and click the mouse button. This establishes the link, and the hyperlink is indicated by its blue colour.

- Remember that if you want to check the link action using Amaya, you will have to double-click the hyperlink.

If you want to make a link to another document, select the word, phrase or image that you want to use as a hyperlink and use the Links icon or the Links — Create link menu. When the pointing hand icon appears, click it over any blank space so that the *Attribute* form appears. Fill in the URL that you want to use and click the *Confirm* button.

**Removing a link or a target**

You can delete an anchor by placing the cursor anywhere in the target (you do not need to select the exact target extent) and using the Links — Delete anchor menu item. This will remove the anchor icon from the position. You can delete a link in the same way, so that the text colour disappears. If you want to change a link so that it points to a different (already created) target, put the cursor in the linking portion and click Links — Change Link, and select the new target.

Amaya contains a vast number of features that have not been described here mainly because they are of little interest to the beginner, and their use requires some experience. If you are likely to move on to designing Web pages for commercial or academic purposes then you should seriously consider Amaya for such uses. A full manual can be downloaded and printed.

# Web site construction simplified

# 4 Creating your Web page

Chapter 3 has dealt with the mechanics of using WYSIWYG editors, and the important topics of how plain text, text effects, tables, lists and pictures can be placed into a page. At first, the page will be saved, using initially a *Save As* command, to a folder on the hard drive, and we will later need to pay attention to how this page file can be transferred to your Web site. This chapter is now concerned with how you create a page with the tools that have been described in chapter 3. First, however, we have to look at the subject of file locations on your hard drive.

**File locations**

You should have created a folder for your files, using some name that will remind you of what it contains. A name such as *JimsWeb* or *MyWeb* is suitable. For a complicated Web site you might need several separate subfolders (one for graphics for example) but for a simple first-effort site we can forget about such complications. This makes it much easier to deal with files that are separate from your main file (usually *index.htm*).

When you insert a picture into a page, you do so by browsing for the picture file. When you use this sort of action with a normal word-processor, you normally have the option to incorporate the picture file into the document (embedding it) or making a link to the picture file (linking it). A Web page always keeps picture files separate so that there is no embedding option; all picture files are linked but the linking action is not obvious in the way that a hyperlink is obvious and visible. The use of linking is what makes it possible to opt for not seeing picture files as you browse.

The consequence of this is that you need to be careful about positioning picture files. Imagine, for example, that you are creating a Web page called *index.htm* in a folder C:\MyWeb.

## Web site construction simplified

You then link in a picture called *Mypix.gif* that is in a folder C:\Pictures\Myset\. This folder information is placed in the HTML code so that when you click on *index.htm* using Windows Explorer or other browser you will see your page and the picture will be loaded from its folder.

That's fine as long as you are working on files stored on your hard drive. When you save your HTML file to your Web site, however, anyone downloading on it will not see the picture, because they have no access to your hard drive. The picture file must be placed in your Web folder, and the link information must be coded so that it can find the picture in this place.

The easiest way to ensure this is to keep picture files in the same folder, MyWeb in this example, and to link them into *index.htm* after they have been placed in the folder. When you do this, the HTML code will refer to the picture as being in the same folder (not in C:\MyWeb), and this instruction is just as valid when the html file and the picture file are both in another folder on a remote Web server computer. This type of reference is called a *relative* reference (or relative addressing), and some WYSIWYG editors will ensure that a relative reference can be used by copying a picture file that has been browsed from a different folder to the folder that you use for your HTML file. Simple editors do not make this provision, and you have to check these things for yourself.

• If you make use of an image file that is on another Web site, then your link has to contain the full URL for that site. This is an *absolute* link (absolute addressing), and at this stage you should try to avoid using such links for pictures, because it results in longer download times.

Complications arise if you want to keep picture files in another folder. For a first simple page, you should not attempt this, but for future reference, you need to know how you can separate files in this way. By far the simplest system is to create a folder that is a subfolder of the one you use for your HTML files, MyWeb in the example. Suppose that you create a subfolder called Pixfiles. A link to a picture called My Dog.gif in this folder would contain the reference \Pixfiles\My Dog.gif. This also is a relative reference which will work when you look at your local *index.htm* using a browser. It will also work on your Web site if you copy the **entire** subfolder Pixfiles to your Web site along with your HTML files.

- If you can keep the organisation of your Web site and your Web folder on your hard drive identical, you will find that you will be free of the annoying common problems that pictures do not appear and pages do not link in.

We'll look at how Web sites can be organised and how files and folders are uploaded in chapter 5.

## Using FPE other templates

When you run FrontPage Express the File — New option shows a number of Wizards and Templates, and we have so far looked at the page that is generated by the Personal Home Page Wizard. You can, however, use a number of other templates and Wizards, but you are not advised to do so until you have had considerable experience. For one thing, these are all intended for more commercial purposes such as gathering information, and for another you would have to check with your IP that your Web site had access to the programs that would allow the actions to work. Since some are for commercial purposes only, you would have to subscribe to commercial Web space in order to use them.

For the sake of completeness, however, we can look first at four possibilities. *Confirmation Form*, *Form Page Wizard*, *New Web View Folder* and *Survey Form*. When you opt for *Confirmation Form*, you will see that this creates a page for the acknowledgement of typed input from a user from *Discussion*, *FormResult* or *Registration* forms.

# Web site construction simplified

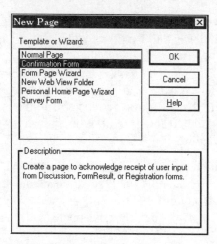

The illustration below shows part of the page that is produced, and since this is intended to service the results from WebBot components in another page, it is unlikely that your IP will allow this material on a normal non-commercial page.

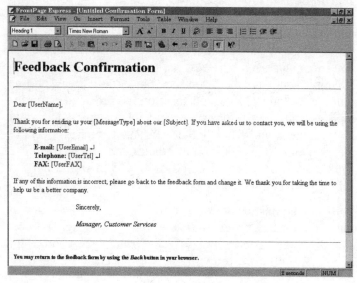

The *Form Page* Wizard allows you to design a form that the user can fill in on screen so that the results can be passed back to you. Once again, the Web site must have access to programs that will handle this data and pass it on to you, and this is unlikely on your free Web space. The illustration shows part of a typical form produced in this way from a list of options provided by the Wizard.

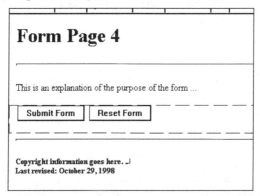

The *New Web View Folder* is used to create a new add-on page, and there are easier ways of doing this. The *Survey Form* is used to gather information from viewers and store it in a file that you can later download and interrogate. Once again, this requires some co-operating at the Web site, though in this case it might be easier to arrange.

**Normal page**

The File — New — Normal page option is the simplest, and it opens up a completely blank page. This is useful if you want to create a page that will be referred to (in a hyperlink, for example) from your index page, and you can fill this page in any of a number of ways:

- by typing text directly into the page,

- by pasting text in from an ASCII text editor,

- by importing text from a word processor file.

## Web site construction simplified

The page can, of course, contains graphics and tables, and you may also want to add bookmarks and hyperlinks, marquees, lines and other items. Such a page will be saved in HTM format to the folder on your hard drive that contains your index.htm file and any other files (such as GIF or JPG) that are associated with your site.

Page creation using FrontPage Express should use the following steps:

1.  Use the *Home Page* Wizard to create a skeleton main page (index.htm) that will be the basis of your site. This page should contain any references to other pages, using hyperlinks that refer to files in the same folder.

2.  Use the *Normal Page* template to create your other pages. These can contain index sections for long pages, pictures, links to other pages.

3.  Ensure that all picture files are held in the same folder as your HTML files, and that the picture insertion has been done from these files.

These steps ensure that you have files on your hard drive that can be transferred to your Web site folder and which will download correctly when you browse and, more important, when anyone else browses.

*   Remember that FrontPage Express can do only a limited amount of work for you. It can create a page that works, but whether it works in the way you want is another thing altogether. Advice on generating pages and checking them is contained in the following section dealing with Word, and you should read the advice contained there also.

### Using Word or other WPs

Creating a page using Word or other word processor is harder work, depending on the facilities in your word processor. If you have Word 97 you can make use of the

Web Wizard (when you opt for a *New* page) and this will create a skeleton index page. This skeleton is not as detailed as the one you can create using the *Home Page* Wizard of FrontPage Express, but it allows you to control the form of your page just as easily.

Because you are using Word, you can import text either from files or by way of cut/copy and paste actions. What you need to remember is that some actions of Word cannot be used, and that others will be converted. These points have been dealt with in chapter 4.

You can create all of your text files in draft form using Word, and save as separate pages in HTML. Once you have all the text files and any picture files in the same folder, you can edit the files, starting with the main index file. You can put in all the hyperlinks you need, using the Insert menu of Word. This is an easier action than the link insertion of some other editors, and you can browse for the files in your main folder.

- Make sure that you have used the spell checker of Word on all of your text. It's embarrassing to have a spelling mistake in a letter, shameful to have it in print, and ridiculous to have it displayed to the whole world. The Word spellchecker is excellent, and easy to use — on Word 97 you can check as you type.

Once the main index file has been completed, with its hyperlinks, open each of your other files in turn, if you are using more than one page. You may want to insert pictures into these pages, so that you need to have the picture files in GIF or JPG format stored in the folder that you use for your Web pages. Once again, you can browse for the picture files and link (not embed) them into the page.

When you have created your HTML pages, close Word and use Internet Explorer to find your Web folder. Click on the main file (*index.htm*) so that Explorer displays it. This is

# Web site construction simplified

what a browser will display when the files are on your Web site, so that what you are seeing is a preview. You have to edit your pages until this view is exactly as you want it.

This is the time to test that all links work. Each link to another page can be checked by clicking it, and if the page does not appear you should make a note to check the link. Each picture should also appear, and if any does not then once again you have to edit the page to find what is wrong with the link.

- Do not expect everything to work absolutely perfectly the first time. If it does, you can congratulate yourself, but if it does not then you will learn more from sorting it out than you would from a table stacked with manuals.

When everything works, print out your pages and look at them critically. Do they convey the information you want the world to see? Are the pictures helpful or a waste of downloading time? Is there a good logical reason for the way that you have split information into different pages or different sections of one long page? Some time spent in this sort of analysis can help to create a much better page.

## Using plain text

If you do not have Word 97 or FrontPage Express, and do not want to download a large program such as AOLpress or Amaya, you can still create Web pages, but with rather more hard work. You will need some software, but it can be simpler software that takes only a few minutes to download.

The software that you will need will be classed as Text to HTML or Text to Web converters. There are many examples available, and a search on the Web will usually produce a new one almost every month. These programs ask you to provide a text source file, and they will then convert it (very quickly) into an HTML file. A typical (and excellent) example is Text2Web from Dev Virdi, available on the site:

http://www.virdi.demon.co.uk/

and this has the advantage of being freeware (unless you upgrade to the Pro version) and with a UK-based author whose e-mail address is included with the software.

The simple version of Text2Web is good for changing text into HTML code, but you cannot expect it to create elaborate tables or links. The Pro version, which is not expensive, is more capable in many respects, but in general you really need something of the order of FrontPage Express if you want to create a page that contains links, tables and such items. You can, however, construct lists, and you can create tables if your text editor can create simple tables.

- You might, however, want to construct a very simple page with no links or pictures, and Text2Web could do this very easily from a text file. It is also very useful for making add-on pages if you have an existing index.htm page.

**Preparing text**

You can prepare suitable text using any text editor, and you can make use of text insertion and pasting of ASCII text as you please. You should preferably use a text editor that supports spell checking. Working from your outline plans, prepare one or more pages of text, save them in TXT format, and then print them. Look critically at the printed version and mark where you want headings with bold text, where you want hyperlinks and where you want pictures eventually to be inserted. Remember that plain text cannot be formatted, so that designing the final appearance of the pages will have to be done on paper.

Now you have to break up your page into sections. A section will contain either plain text, a list or a table, because Text2Web uses different commands for different layouts. Save your text sections and your list sections as separate

## Web site construction simplified

files. You can then convert each section into HTML, and then join up the HTML files by reading the first file into a text editor and then adding in the others in order, finally saving the result with a suitable filename such as index.htm.

When your text files have been saved you can convert them to HTML using Text2Web. Start Text2Web and specify the Layout option as Smart format. This is the best setting for a piece of plain text, which is what your first piece of text will probably be. You now need to specify input and output.

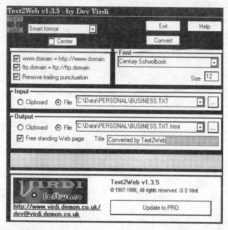

For some purposes, you can use the Clipboard as both input and output. If you cut or copy text from a text file (which can be a long text file), you can specify the clipboard for both input and output so that after you have clicked the *Convert* button you will have the HTML code in your clipboard. You can now paste this into a blank open text file, allowing you to repeat these actions to build up a complete HTML file.

The alternative is to name separate files for both input and output, and if you want more than a small amount of simple text this is probably a better option because you are less likely to become mixed up as to what kind of content you have on your Clipboard at any given time. You can click the button next to the filename space (marked with dots) to browse for a folder and file).

- If you tick the box marked *Free standing Web page*, the output will be a separate HTML file. This is ideal for creating a new index file or a new page, and you can use the *Title* space to type a filename for the HTML page. If you are inserting more HTML code into an existing file, remove the tick on this box and use output to the Clipboard.

When you convert text that contains lists or tables, you need to choose the appropriate *Output* format. The *Smart* format is intended for simple text files that do not contain any lists or tables, nothing in which row or column position is important. With this option, Text2Web will determine the layout format.

- For a text document that contains a simple list, you should use the option called *Retain original linefeeds*.

- For a text document that contains tables, use the *Retain original format* option. Remember that if you create tables in a simple text editor you should use a monospaced font such as Courier.

- You can generate bulleted or numbered lists if you use the *HTML List* option.

- The Pro version contains options for *HTML Table* and *Links Selection Box*.

## HTML editors

The use of an HTML editor is not so difficult for a beginner to Web site construction as you might imagine. The point about such an editor is that it does not require you to know all the HTML codes, it allows you to insert codes by pointing and clicking for the effect that you want on selected text. This is, in fact, easier to use for more elaborate pages

# Web site construction simplified

than a text converter. Another advantage of the HTML type of editor is that it can be small and compact, quicker to download and taking up less space on your hard drive than a full-blown WYSIWYG editor. One of the best-known small HTML editors is HotDog from Sausage Software (Australia) which can be downloaded from a number of sites — try a search on the word HotDog, or the main site at:

http://www.sausage.com

- Note that HotDog is a form of text editor, so that you do not need any other software to create a Web page. There is, however, no spelling checker, so that you might want to use another text editor to fill that particular gap. You will need to have a browser program if you want to see what your document looks like in final form.

When HotDog opens, you will see a screen that is very similar to that of a word processor, except that some HTML code has been created in advance. This is the minimum code that exists for any HTML file, and your own text must be placed in the space between the lines with <BODY> and </BODY>.

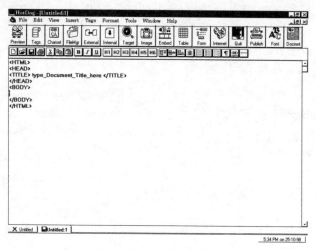

84

You can now type or paste in some text. HotDog will accept text that has been pasted from a word processor, but this will always appear as plain text, with no effects like font variations, bold, italic, etc. You can also import text from a file using the Insert — Text file menu. This text should be plain ASCII text, not a word-processor file such as a DOC file of Word.

- If you use a word-processor file you will see a large number of strange characters appearing. These are the word-processor formatting codes, but HotDog imports them as if they were plain text characters.

You can use the Return key to create a new paragraph, and enter text until you come to require some other element, such as a list, table, picture, etc. These can then be entered using the facilities of HotDog.

You can use either the small icons or the Insert menu for these insertions. The icons are clear enough, and there are ToolTips used to indicate the effect of each icon. The formatting icons consist of *Bold*, *Italic*, and *Underlined* followed by *Headers* of levels 1 to 6. There are three image alignment icons, one for centring text, and icons that will start the three main types of list. The last three icons will insert a paragraph, insert a line break or insert a horizontal line.

The large icons are labelled as *Preview*, *Tags*, *Charset*, *FileMgr*, *External*, *Internal*, *Target*, *Image*, *Embed*, *Table*, *Form*, *Internet*, *Quit*, *Publish*, *Font* and *Docmnt*. Each will show a ToolTip when the cursor is placed over the icon.

Another approach is to use the Insert menu, illustrated following. This menu contains all the items that are available in icon form and shows short-cut keys for many items.

# Web site construction simplified

| | |
|---|---|
| Image... | |
| Image (Advanced)... | Ctrl+M |
| Embedded Item... | Ctrl+E |
| Form Element... | |
| Hypertext Target... | Ctrl+G |
| Table... | Ctrl+T |
| List... | Ctrl+L |
| Horizontal Line... | |
| Text File... | |
| Special | ▸ |
| Simple URL... | F4 |
| Jump to a Document in this System... | Ctrl+J |
| Jump to a Document on Another System... | Ctrl+H |
| Jump Within this Document... | Ctrl+K |
| Launch an Internet Service... | Ctrl+Y |

The important difference between using HotDog or any other HTML editor and the types we looked at in chapter 3, is that HotDog shows only the code. When you insert a picture using FrontPage Express, you will see the picture appear. When you insert a picture using HotDog you will see only HTML code, such as:

<EMBED SRC="../pix/hotdog~1.gif">

and this gives you no idea of how the page will look. For that reason, HotDog has a *Preview* icon, and when you first press this you will be asked to find the EXE file for your browser. Once you have located this (such as iexplore.exe) then the icon for that browser will replace the default Preview icon.

That point apart, HotDog is very easy to use, and in the 30 days that you are given to evaluate you should be able to form an opinion on what value you get for your registration of $29.95 or equivalent. If you feel, as many do, that it is preferable to see the HTML code as you create it, then the use of HotDog or a similar HTML editor is desirable.

## Adding other items

FrontPage Express and many other editors provide for adding items that are far removed from normal text, so that you can add buttons, text boxes, drop-down boxes, reply forms and so on.

These all sound very interesting, but they are intended for use in a commercial Web site, and their use is not straightforward.

For example, suppose you insert a button into your document, This is easy enough, no matter what type of editor you use, but what will it do? A preview of your code using a browser will not indicate any action, because at a local level there is none. Any action that a button or similar element will have when the files are placed on the Web site will depend on what programs are provided on the Web site by the IP. On a home-user site there might be only a few such programs available, or even none. Very often a counter program is provided so that your Web page can show how many times it has been looked at, but you can find this type of information only by asking your IP.

- Your IP may indicate that some files can be downloaded to your hard drive folder so that you can check their action locally. This is very convenient, but it is not always possible.

- In particular, only a limited number of IPs will be able to use the WebBots of FrontPage Express, and you should not use any of these devices in your Web page unless your IP confirms that they will be recognised.

# Web site construction simplified

# 5 Uploading and changing

All that we have done so far is concerned with the creation of material for a Web page and its storage in a local folder in the form of HTML and GIF files. We now have to look at how these files can be placed on your own Web space. As usual, there are several methods and some are much easier to use than others.

- Whatever methods you use, your aim should be to make the contents of your allocated Web folder identical to the contents of the folder on your hard drive that contains your HTML and GIF files. This is by far the best way of ensuring that you keep close control of your Web pages.

The essential preliminary to all this is to establish what URL is needed for your own site. This URL will consist of an address for the IP and a portion, usually following a forward slash, that indicates your own personal space. Your own IP will provide this information, and the examples in this book are drawn from the methods used by Globalnet. Another major provider was asked to indicate its methods, but did not reply to my e-mail.

**Case sensitivity**

The next essential is to check all of your files and hyperlinks for the use of upper and lower case. You soon become so used to the fact that Windows regards a file called *Image1.gif* as being identical to one called *image1.gif* that you cannot imagine any other option.

The large computers that are used as Web servers by IP companies, however, are most unlikely to use Windows. They will, in all probability, be using an older form of operating system called *Unix*. *Unix* uses names that are always case-sensitive, so that *Image1* is not the same as *image1*, and this causes problems with files that have been written using Windows software.

## Web site construction simplified

The main problem is that Editors, whether HTML or WYSIWYG, and the FTP programs that are often used to upload Web files, all try to convert filenames to lower case. If, for example, you have named a file in your local Web folder *Mypix1.gif*, then when this is uploaded to your (remote) Web site it will appear as *mypix1.gif*. That's fine, but your document's HTML code probably still contains a reference that links into *Mypix1.gif*, and this is not the same. Conversion of file names is all very well, but since filenames used within HTML code are not converted, this can make a problem when there was not one earlier.

The agreed convention is to use only lower-case, avoiding capital letters in any filenames or links with filenames. If you rigorously check your documents and ensure that all filenames or filename references are in lowercase then you are not likely to experience trouble on this score.

- If, however, you view your Web site using a browser and find that some pictures do not appear or that a hyperlink jump does not happen, then this is the most likely explanation.

This is a good reason for using an FTP program for maintaining your site, because it allows you to see the names of files on your site and even to change them. Details of using FTP will follow in this chapter

## Save As

The simplest way of uploading a file to your Web site is to open the file in your Editor (WYSIWYG or HTML) and then use the File — Save As menu item. When the panel appears, fill in the URL for your Web site and click the OK button. On FrontPage Express, for example, the *Save As* panel is intended by default to save to the remote Web site, and you have to click on the *As File* button if you want to save locally to your hard drive.

Other editors offer variations on this theme. AOLpress offers a *Sites* line in the *Save As* panel so that you can enter the site for AOL Web space as:

http://members.aol.com/screen_name

where *screen_name* represents the code word for your own piece of Web space. You can also fill in an address into the *Location space*, such as:

http://members.aol.com/screen_name/mypage.htm

for AOL users to put in a file called, in this example, mypage.htm.

Amaya uses a *Save As* panel that allows a browse button for local files and expects you to type the full URL for your Web space into the *Document* location space. You can also specify a location for image files, if this is different.

HotDog has a *Publishing* icon, but this saves files to a local folder, and you are expected to use an FTP program for uploading.

## FTP

FTP means File Transfer Protocol, and FTP is a set of rules (making up a *protocol*) that have been established for exchanging files between computers. FTP was the first protocol that was established in the 1960s for the Internet and it is still the standard for this action. All modern browsers, such as Microsoft Internet Explorer, allow for the use of FTP to transfer program files. The thing that makes FTP important for Web site authors is that it also makes it possible to upload files to a remote Web site.

### Browsing and file transfer

Computers on the Internet (or on a local network) can communicate with each other by making use of several different protocols. As noted earlier, these protocols are sets

# Web site construction simplified

of rules that ensure both computers use the same codes for the same actions; they *speak the same language*.

The World Wide Web uses HTTP (Hypertext Text Transfer Protocol), which is why so many Web sites URLs start with http://. E-mail and newsgroups make use of their own protocols, and FTP is yet another Internet protocol, different from these used for browsing, e-mail or news.

Using the browsing protocol, you locate a site by using the URL that consists of three portions. The first portion shows what protocol is being used, and for browsing this is http://. If you were using FTP protocol, you would type a URL that started with ftp://. The second part of a URL locates the computer that holds the files you want to see, and a typical example would be www.global.net.co.uk/. The last part is the name and path for a file on that computer, and it uses slash signs to separate folders, for example /home/benefits.

When you use a modern browser, the http:// portion will be filled in for you, so that you need only type the part of the URL that starts with www. Most Internet users know this, but fewer know that any file with the name *index.htm* will also be automatically recognised, so that you need not type this name if you want the index file on any computer — you can type a URL such as www.global.net.uk and you will see the index file (or home page) without needing to specify it.

When you want to make transfers in either direction, you use the FTP form of URL. The only difference in most cases is that this URL starts with ftp:// in place of http://, and when you add the computer part of the address you will be taken to the main (root) folder for files. If your software is good, then you can browse around the files on the server as easily as you can browse files using Windows Explorer.

One problem in the past has been that most FTP software is of ancient origin, written in the days when operating a computer was a skill that few people ever acquired. Software of that type is still used by professionals, often because it allows for actions that only professionals need, but the average modern computer user, accustomed to Windows, expects something that is more visual and easier to use, making use of mouse pointing and clicking rather than requiring command codes to be typed.

Browsing through the file display using FTP is very fast, because you do not download any files until you want to, and the amount of downloading needed to show the display of files and folders is minimal. When you browse the Web, you do so by connecting to a server and then retrieving files which are then displayed by the web browser. You can then use links on a browsed file to download other pages and so on, but you always have to move from one page to another, downloading each one. When you use FTP, you connect to the server, select your file from the list, and download only what you want. You do not see the content of a file, because FTP is used for downloading program files rather than reading pages. Using FTP, all the files that exist on the remote computer and are available for public use are available to you. Some FTP sites are restricted (by password) to subscribers only.

From the beginning, mainly because of the military origins of the Internet, the protocol needs a user name and a password to log in to a remote site. You will still use this process when you upload your own pages to your Web site, because this prevents anyone else from altering your site. In the course of the development of the Internet, however, the idea of anonymous logging in developed. This uses the name *anonymous* as the user name and your e-mail address as the password for all sites. FTP software will use this system automatically, so that you will have access automatically to all public FTP sites without needing to type user information.

# Web site construction simplified

With all that information to work on, let's look now at methods for uploading your Web files to the server, with a brief glimpse at how to download program files such as browsers, editors and other useful software.

## Web Publishing Wizard

The Web Publishing Wizard is part of Internet Explorer 4, and is a specialised FTP program for uploading files to a Web site. You should find the program WPWIZ.EXE in the Web Publish folder which is normally in the Program Files folder of your hard drive. If you do not find it there, use a search for wpwiz.exe on your hard drive. If the program has been installed correctly, then it will be available by using Start — Programs — Internet Explorer unless you have re-organised your Start menu.

When you start the Wizard, you will see an introductory panel. This carries the message:

> Welcome to Microsoft Web Publishing Wizard. This wizard helps you publish your Web pages, support files, and other Web content files on a Web server. The Web server can be located on your local area network (LAN) or it can be maintained by your Internet service provider (ISP).
>
> The wizard needs information about your Web pages, support files, and your Web server. If you don't have this information, contact your system administrator or ISP.
>
> To begin publishing your Web pages, click Next.

You now have time to gather all the information that you need, such as the path to the folder that contains your files

and the URL for uploading files to your Web site.
Remember that you have to activate your site (send a
message to the IP that you need space set aside for you).

When you click the *Next* button you will see the first main
panel of the Wizard.

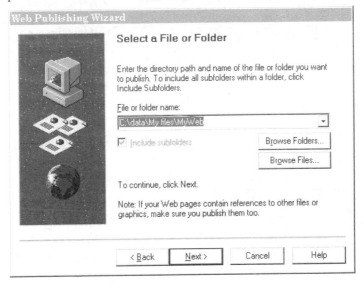

This asks for the name of the folder that contains your files,
or the name of a file you want to upload. If your first effort
is only a single page, usually called *index.htm*, then you can
specify this filename along with the path. If you don't want
to type the path, then you can use either of the buttons
marked *Browse for Folders* or *Browse for Files*. If you use a
folder, then all the files in that folder will be uploaded when
the last stage of the Wizard is reached.

- The box marked *Include subfolders* is usually ticked by
  default to ensure that any subfolders (for example, used
  for GIF files) will be uploaded.

When you click the *Next* button on this panel, you will see
the next step of the Wizard, which calls for you to enter the

## Web site construction simplified

URL for your Web site. This has to be the full URL, which will include your user name incorporated as part of the final folder name.

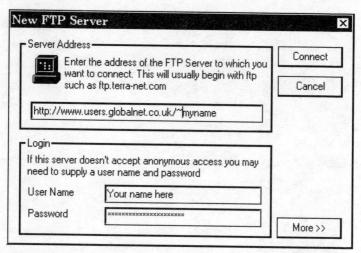

This URL is the information that you need from your IP, and the example shows the form of the URL for publishing to a Global Internet site. When you click the *Next* button you will see a *Publish Your Files* notice, and clicking *Finish* on that panel will make contact with the IP so that the files can be uploaded.

The Web Publishing Wizard is a simple piece of software, and you might have uploaded your files by this time using a *Save As* command in your Web Editor program. If you are doubtful about the steps, however, the use of a Wizard is very reassuring. Note that the Wizard illustrated here is the Windows 98 version, and you will find differences in earlier versions.

### Using Terrapin FTP

Terrapin FTP is a superb FTP program that runs under Windows and uses Windows methods. An early version is available on the Global FTP site, and you can download samples from other sites also. For the most recent version you should download from:

http://www.terra-net.com

— note that this is the browser site, but you can download from this or the corresponding FTP site.

Terrapin uses the same form of display and navigation as Windows Explorer, and its dual-window displays both your local hard drive and the remote Web site so that you can drag folders and files from one to the other. This is by far the simplest system for FTP that I have seen, and made the registration fee for Terrapin a decided bargain.

• One very useful feature is that if a transfer is interrupted it can be resumed later when connection is re-established. This is particularly useful if you are downloading large program files.

**Terrapin uploading**

Before you use Terrapin or any other uploading software you should make certain as far as possible that your pages are working correctly when you browse them from your hard drive. This is easy to check if, as has been strongly recommended, you keep all of your files in the same folder. You can develop the use of a sub-folder as you gain experience.

• Some items, such as hit counters, that depend on program files at the Web site, cannot be tested locally.

Once you are sure that everything that can be tested locally is working correctly you can gather the information for uploading. You need, mainly, the URL for the FTP server that contains your web site, complete with the extension that identifies your own part of the Web space.

You can now start Terrapin. When you see the screen appear the setting will be for working offline, because once you

# Web site construction simplified

have used Terrapin for uploading or downloading, it retains a record of the file structure at the Web server.

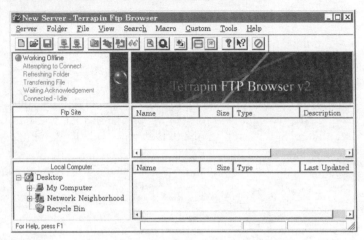

Terrapin uses two panels, of which the upper panel shows the remote site and the lower panel shows your hard drive. Each panel uses the Explorer style of display for folders and files. You now need to connect with your server using Terrapin so that Terrapin will capture an Explorer view of the Web site.

1.  Click on Server – New Connection. You will see the *New FTP Server* pane appear.

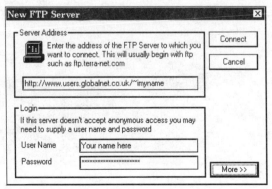

2. Fill in the site URL, using the full address that your IP has specified. You do not normally need to fill in anything in the name and password sections because these will be entered automatically.

3. Click the *Connect* button. Once this has been done, your server will appear in the Server list so that you do not need to supply this information again.

4. You will see the remote Web site folders and file appear — this illustration shows files already in the public_html folder of the server.

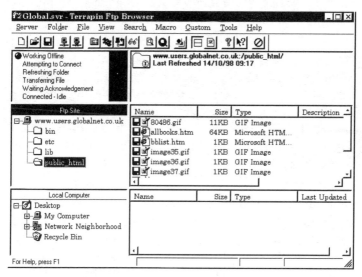

5. You should now locate your folder and files on your hard drive, using the lower panel.

6. Now click on your folder or select files and drag them across to the server. You need to take some care over this because you probably don't want the folder name (such as MyWeb) to be transferred, only the files it contains. If you have named your local folder on the hard drive to the same name as is used on the server

(public_html in this example) then there is no harm in dragging the whole folder.

- Do not be afraid to experiment, because for as long as you are connected you can delete a file in the server just as easily as you can delete a file locally.

- If you drag a new version of a file, the remote files display will not show the change until you select the remote folder and press the F5 (Refresh) key.

You have now uploaded your Web pages, and you can check this by clicking the remote folder (public_html in this example) and using the menu item Folder — Refresh or clicking on the *Folder Refresh* tool. You should be able to see all your Web files, including the graphics files.

When you leave Terrapin you will be prompted to *Save Site Map.* This is a very useful feature, because it stores on your hard drive a copy of this view of the Web site, so that you can see the site even when you are offline. This makes it very simple to check if there is any difference between the local folder and the one that has been placed on the Web site.

Can you browse your site with Internet Explorer now? A lot depends on your IP. My experience was that as soon as I had shut down Terrapin I was able to use IE4 to see a browser view of my site (and record the first hit!). Some IPs will not make your site available for a day or two and you simply have to wait and keep trying.

**Site maintenance**

Uploading to your site is seldom the end of it all, because any site needs to be maintained. You may need to update information, add items you did not think of earlier, put in some links to sites that interest you, and add some appreciative comments on local items of interest. Much of the work of updating, however, is concerned with improving the appearance of the site and making it easier to find in a search.

You should always make any updating to your local files to start with. This makes sure that what you are adding will work, so that you do not land up with egg on your face because of a change that causes problems, a link that goes nowhere or a picture that does not display.

- Remember that a picture may not display for two main reasons. One is that the picture is not in the correct folder or that the link is wrong; the other is that you have used uppercase in a filename. In the first example, you should be able to find the problem locally, in the second you don't see it unless you are browsing the site.

Once you have made all your changes locally and checked them out as far as possible, you can drag the updated files (and possibly some new files) to the server site. When you complete a transfer of files in this way you will see a panel with an *Options* button. Click on this to see options, including the option *Upload files only if newer*. This is a useful option because it allows you always to drag the whole set of files knowing that only the altered or new files will be transferred, saving time. You can also select the first five options to ensure that Terrapin will always ensure that your remote site contains exactly the same files as your local folder.

## Other FTPs

Terrapin is by no means the only FTP program that you can use for uploading and maintaining your Web site files, though you may have gathered that I think it worth considering. In addition, there is no space in this book to illustrate the uses of FTP for downloading program files and since this is an action that is well described elsewhere we shall omit it.

## Web site construction simplified

There are other FTP programs you might like to consider, though, and possibly try out for yourself. One is FTP Explorer which is free for home or educational users. It can be downloaded from

**http://www.ftpx.com**

or

**ftp://ftp.ftpx.com/pub/ftpx/ftpx.zip**

- If you download a zip file you will have to extract it before you can make use of the program files.

You install FTP Explorer by unzipping the distribution file and running the Setup.exe program by clicking on it in Windows Explorer — you can also use the Start — Run option if Setup.exe is in a convenient folder. You will be asked for a folder location and you can pick the default or type another path, then click the *Next* button to start the copying action. You will be asked about installing Start button options and placing shortcuts on the Desktop. You may need to reboot your computer, depending on the options you have chosen.

Once the reboot is complete you can launch FTP Explorer.

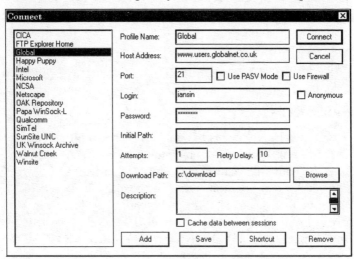

The illustration here shows the appearance of the opening *Connect* screen once a server has been installed. The Global server has been added by using the *New* button, so that to start an FTP session you need only click the *Connect* button.

• Note that the list of servers includes several well-known FTP sites, so that this can be very useful if you are looking for software to download.

When you connect, you will, after all the connections have been made, see a screen similar to the illustration below.

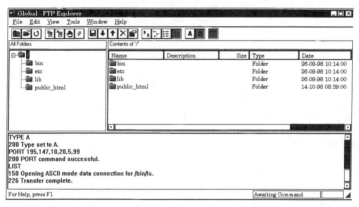

This is geared to exploring the remoter server mainly, devoting all of the screen space to this. Once you have found the folder you want, you can click the arrow buttons that are labelled *Upload* and *Download*, according to which action you want to carry out. You will then see a new pane appear with an Explorer view of your hard drive so that you can select a folder for uploading or for downloaded files.

**WS_FTP**

WS_FTP is another FTP program (from Ipswitch of Lexington, Mass.) that is free for a home or educational user, and it can be downloaded from the manufacturer's site:

**http://www.ipswitch.com**

# Web site construction simplified

or you can search for WS_FTP to find nearer sites. You can usually get a fast download from the main site in the morning, but it can become slower later in the day. The main program is currently WSFTP95.exe

When you set up WS_FTP and start the program running you will see the *Session Properties* panel appear over the main display, as illustrated.

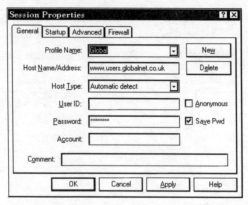

As shown here this has already been set up for a Global connection and all the details needed for your connection will be shown. If you are running WS_FTP for the first time you will need to click the *Connect* button in order to fill in the details of your IP.

Once you have made connection, you will see the main screen of WS_FTP. This, like Terrapin, uses a screen that is divided into local and remote sections, and the local set will show by default the files in the WS_FTP folder. The illustration, following, shows only the local folder, because there is no provision for storing the remote folder information.

There is a set of file control buttons on the right-hand side of each display, and the button labels are:

| | |
|---|---|
| **ChgDir** | Used to change to another folder |
| **MkDir** | Used to create another folder |
| **\*.\*** | Show all files |
| **View** | View contents of a selected file |
| **Exec** | Run a selected program file |
| **Rename** | Rename a selected file |
| **Delete** | Delete a selected file |
| **Refresh** | Refresh file display |
| **DirInfo** | Show extended data on files |

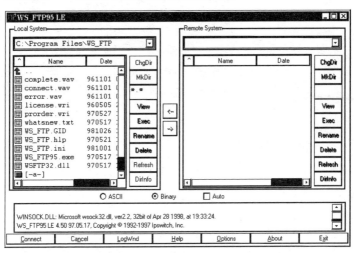

If a file is not selected, only a few items are available, and the others are greyed out as indicated by the blurred names in the illustration.

The action of WS_FTP is so similar to that of Terrapin in the way that it uses the two panels that it is pointless to describe the actions in detail. Transferring files is done by selecting files in one side and then clicking on the arrow icons between the panels, depending on which direction of transfer you want to use.

The whole action is controlled by the buttons that appear in the illustration, so that no menu bar is used. The Options button leads to a large number of tabs for configuring WS_FTP to your own requirements.

# 6 Making it known

The usual aim of establishing a Web site is to broadcast to the entire world that you exist, and let them all know what you do, think, know, or work at. For some users, this might not seem desirable, and if you make no effort to place your site on a search list, then no-one but you, and selected people you communicate with, will ever know.

- You might imagine that search engines looked in computers all over the world to find what was stored there. This is fanciful — even at modern computing speeds there would never be time for this. All that search engines do is to store a list of key words along with a URL for each site that is notified to them. If you don't notify them they don't know you.

For the rest of us, quite glad to get in touch with everyone in this way, uploading files and checking the site has to be followed by ensuring that anyone carrying out a search will find you. This is by no means as easy as you might think mainly because of the different ways in which search engines work.

## Searching

Most of the search engines that you see on your browser are located in the US, and the best-known are Lycos and Alta Vista. There are, however, a large number of lesser-known engines, and some are linked so that an entry added to one is automatically added to some others. In addition, there are agencies that will add your URL to a number of search engines.

Before you start tapping keys, stop to think what a search engine will identify. Suppose your Web page consists only of the file *index.htm*, as many do. The main heading on your page is called *My Home Page*. What will a search engine make of this?

## Web site construction simplified

The answer is that it will show the page either as *My Home Page* or as *index.htm*, and so far, that's not something that anyone is likely to search for. You may find other information, depending on sub-headings, or text immediately below the main heading, you have used.

Take some time to look at what other Web authors have done. The usual scheme is to think of keywords that a searcher might use. For example, if you want to advertise skills or interests in model cars, photos of aircraft, programming in Visual Basic and motor bikes, then you should put suitable key words into your index.htm page, as close to the main heading as possible. You might also want to put your name into the main heading.

This might prompt you to re-design your index page, and that's the reason for the methods that have been described for designing and constructing this page. You can make the alterations on your local copy, and then upload the new version, so that when you spread the word to the search engines there is a chance that someone will find you from your work.

### Search engines

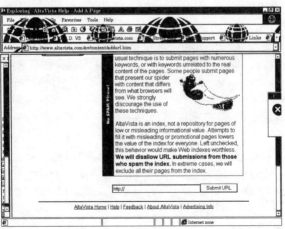

Typically, you can make contact with a search engine through a browser. Somewhere in the main page of the search engine there will be a reference to placing your site into the list. Part of a typical form, in this case from Alta Vista, is shown here.

This has been obtained by clicking the *Add a page* item at the foot of the Alta Vista opening page. The text that appears on this page presents such good advice that it is worth quoting:

> Please submit only one URL. Our crawler, Scooter, will eventually explore your entire site by following links. If the page is successfully fetched, it is added to the index. It should be available for queries typically in less than a day, possibly two days for our mirror sites.

> Do not submit a description or keywords with a URL. To control the abstract served back with your page, use META tags. Remember that URLs are case-sensitive, and please check your spelling. We also accept submissions of URLs through Scott Banister's Submit It! service and Net Creations PostMaster services. Subscribe your company name, trademarks, brand names and slogans to the Real Name System.

> Removing Pages or URLs from the Index

> To remove a bad link from the index, simply resubmit the URL. All URLs that return a status code of 404 ("Not Found") are removed from the index within a day or two of being submitted.

> To remove a page that does exist from the index, it will be necessary to write a robots.txt file for the site.

# Web site construction simplified

> To exclude all pages of a site from the index, it will be necessary to write a robots.txt file for the site.
>
> A small number of sites regularly submit a large number of pages to the Alta Vista index in the hope of showing very frequently on our result pages. The usual technique is to submit pages with numerous keywords, or with keywords unrelated to the real content of the pages.
>
> Some people submit pages that present our spider with content that differs from what browsers will see. We strongly discourage the use of these techniques.
>
> Alta Vista is an index, not a repository for pages of low or misleading informational value. Attempts to fill it with misleading or promotional pages lowers the value of the index for everyone. Left unchecked, this behavior would make Web indexes worthless. We will disallow URL submissions from those who spam the index. In extreme cases, we will exclude all their pages from the index.

The reference to meta-tags is worth exploring further because this provides additional ways for ensuring that key words are found in a search. The normal action of Alta Vista is to index all the words in the page, and to use the first few words as a short abstract which shows up when a search result is listed.

You can, however, exercise some control over the indexing process by altering the HTML codes in your page, and this is what the name *Meta tags* refers to. In this case, you add a line that starts with <META. For example if you added:

<META name="description"

content="I specialise in writing text on computers. ">

then this phrase would be used in the abstract. You can also use a META line to add keywords:

<META name="keywords" content="technical writing, UK, Computers, Electronics">

Since META is a recognised part of HTML code, this action should apply to any search engine. You can add HTML codes directly using any type of editor, WYSIWYG or HTML. For example, in FrontPage Express, you can add HTML at any point in a page by using the Insert — HTML Markup menu item.

- Note that there is no way to check the action of this type of line locally, but you should check that it does not appear when you browse.

You might wonder how long it will take for your added page to feature in a search. There is no simple answer, because some engines use a highly automated system that adds your page almost immediately, others go through a checking process so that it can take up to a week before you can do a search on words that you know are unique to your page and find it from the search results.

- In my case, I also found several other Ian Sinclairs, none directly related.

Not all search engines are so obliging as to have an add URL section, and you can look at UK Plus until you are blue in the face looking for a way to enter a page. This brings us to the use of the services that will carry out such entries. These are usually free for the small-time Web user, though they will levy a fee on commercial organisations. One of the foremost services is Submit-It!, another is Net Creations PostMaster service.

## Web site construction simplified

- There is also the Real Name System which should be used for items such as company name, trademarks, brand names and slogans.

### Using Submit-It!

The branch of Submit-It! that you need for a personal page is Submit-It! Free and is at the site:

http://siteowner.linkexchange.com/

When you go to this site you will see forms for submitting a site, for inspecting your site, and for adding Meta tags to your page.

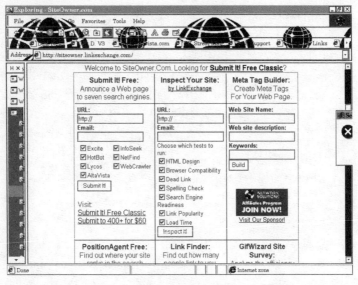

The listed search engines are Excite, HotBot, Lycos, AltaVista, InfoSeek, NetFnd and WebCrawler. These are all main sites and most of the search actions that are carried out each day will use one of another of these US-based engines.

You are asked to enter the URL for your site, and your e-mail address into the form, and you can then click the *Submit* button to enter your page into the listings. The entry can take time, and some engines take longer than others, so that you should allow a week before you can expect all the sites you have listed to be able to find your page from a search for keywords (such as your name).

The other parts of the *Submit* page are also useful. You can opt to check the design of your page or to insert meta tags that will allow you to determine the contents of an abstract or to add keywords. There are also facilities for finding where your site is placed on different search engines when you provide a keyword, and for finding if any pages have links to yours.

There is another site of similar nature at:

http://end2.bedrock.com/submit.html

and this uses a separate form for each search engine — a few are illustrated here:

**List-based WWW Catalogs**

Yahoo
**Category:**
**Title:**
**URL:**
| Submit It! to Yahoo | Clear this form |

EINet Galaxy
**Title:**
**URL:**
| Submit It! to EINet Galaxy | Clear this form |

Project DA-CLOD
**Title:**
**URL:**
| Submit It! to Project DA-CLOD | Clear this form |

The entry method is much the same, but the range of sites includes some smaller search engines that you might not have come across.

# Web site construction simplified

## Checking for your entry

Submitting an entry does not mean that it will appear instantly on a search engine. It may appear within a day on a few, within a week on others, and not at all on some. The only way that you can be sure that your site is being included is by searching for it yourself, using the search engines that are available from your own server and searching for a set of words that are likely to be unique to your Web site. If you find on a search for your name, for example, that you turn up some 4,000 pages you obviously need to make your search more specific to your site.

This is where differences between search engines become glaring obviously. Many types assume that if you make a search for *Ian Sinclair author* that you are looking for a page that contains all three of these words, and that's true of several search engines. In others you might have to phrase this search as *Ian+Sinclair+author*, and several searches will look for any of the words you supply unless you use this format. If you find that a search keeps turning up pages that include only one of your words, then try the search using the + signs in the search line. If all else fails, try reading the advice that each search site offers on how to specify your search more precisely.

Whatever you do, please do not flood the Net with copies of your page using slightly different words. Some artists, for example, use one basic page but make many copies, each one carrying the title of a different painting or subject. A search for that artist will then show a page for each work, rather than the option of clicking on a link in the home page to see a list if subjects and titles. This sort of thing overloads the search engines, and some will eventually remove all but one reference.

114

# 7 HTML guide

I promised at the start of this book that you would not need to know how to work with HTML code in order to create your own Web site, and I have kept the promise. If your requirements remain simple, so that the Web site you have created for yourself suits your needs, then you need read no further. If, however, you feel that you would like to know more, to be able to put effects into your site that can't be handled by the editor you are using, or if you feel that you would like to get into this work for a living, this chapter deals with the code that your editor has produced, HTML.

HTML is a coding system that is based on styles of display that are independent of the type of computer you use to create or read the documents. This is important, because it allows any type of computer to make use of the net, and when you exchange HTML files with another computer you cannot tell what machine is at the other end of the connection.

- HTML was invented by Tim Berners-Lee while he was working at CERN, the European Laboratory for Particle Physics in Geneva.

The description here is based on Version 4.0 of HTML. As HTML develops there will be new versions, but any code that has been written for an older version will still be valid for the later versions. Only new codes are added, the old ones remain valid.

- This is not an exhaustive guide to HTML, only an introduction that is intended to show what it is all about. It covers as much as you would need to know in order to create simple Web sites or to understand the coding produced by programs such as FrontPage Express.

## Web site construction simplified

The important point about HTML is that it uses only characters that are in the ASCII plain text set. This is why HTML documents can be used with any type of computer and why they can be created with any plain text editor, or by using the *plain text with line breaks* option of a word processor.

### Elements and tags

When you think of how a document is constructed, you normally think of items such as the ordinary paragraph text, the headings of various levels, pictures, captions, tables, lists and so on. These are the elements of the document, and HTML uses markers called tags to indicate what type of element is being used at any particular part of a document. These tags are normally used in pairs, so that one tag marks the start of an element (perhaps the first letter of the first word in a heading) and another tag marks the end of the element (the last letter in the heading, for example).

Since these tags must use normal ASCII codes, the angle brackets (< >) are selected for this purpose because they don't appear in many documents as part of the normal text. A complete tag consists of an opening angle bracket, a short tag name, and a closing angle bracket. For example, the tag to start a level 1 heading is <H1>, and the forward slash mark is used to show an ending tag, so that the end of a heading would be marked as </H1>. We'll list a set of HTML tags later.

Suppose you need to use angle brackets (and also the & character) in your text? Because of their use in HTML coding you cannot simply type these characters as text, and you have to use codes such as &lt, &gt, &amp for these signs. These are called *escape sequences*.

- HTML tag names can be in upper or lower case, so that you can normally use <h1> of <H1> interchangeably.

116

There are some exceptions to this for the tags called *escape sequences.*

In addition to a tag name, some starting tags need to contain additional information called *attributes.* A typical attribute is one that would be used to align an image (with attributes of top, middle or bottom).

Most browsers will follow the HTML use of tags exactly. If, however, your browser does not recognise a particular tag, it will show whatever text is placed between the start and end tags of a document. This allows for a new version of HTML to be used along with browsers that are geared to an older version.

**Head and body**

Even before any text is put into an HTML document, some standard tags must be present, as illustrated here.

```
<HTML>
<HEAD>
<TITLE> Text of title</TITLE>
</HEAD>
<BODY>
Document text in here
</BODY>
</HTML>
```

Each document is identified as the characters lying between the <HTML> and </HTML> tags, and consists of head and body text. The head contains the title, marked by tags at each end, and the body contains the actual text that is made up of headings, paragraphs, pictures, lists, tables and other elements. Browsers can cope with HTML only if this format of layout is strictly observed.

- HTML editors such as HotDog will put in these standard essential parts for you, and if you create HTML text

# Web site construction simplified

using a simple text editor you can use a template that contains these elements already.

### Looking at a file

Take a look at a longer document for yourself. Download a Web page, preferably one that is not too fancy in design, and take a look at the code. If you use Internet Explorer, for example, you can use the menu item View — Source, and other browsers have similar ways of viewing the HTML for a document. The illustration shows part of an example treated in this way — note that Internet Explorer calls up NotePad to display the HTML file.

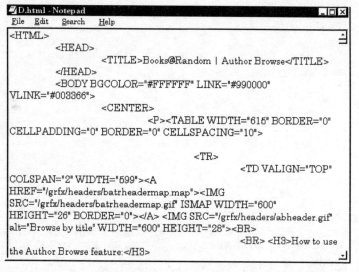

You do not need to understand all that you see to appreciate the way that tags are used, and you can find out how to carry out effects that you want to use in your own work by looking at the HTML code in these examples — remember that you can copy and paste HTML just as you can any other text.

## Tag list

What follows is a list of currently-used HTML tags in their start format. The end tag is be identical apart from the slash sign. The first set of tags shown here are essential for each document. Some attributes have been omitted because they are not essential to the newcomer to HTML.

<HTML>

This tag is essential and is used as an instruction to the browser that the file consists of data that has been coded in HTML format. Your browser will expect this tag to be used for any file that uses the extension of htm or html.

<HEAD>

Another essential tag that is used to identify the head part of the HTML document, which is the part that contains the title that will appear in your Browser.

<TITLE>

This tag starts the words used for the title of a page. This title is displayed by the browser and is also identified by a search engine. You should keep a title short, certainly less than 64 characters.

<BODY>

The body of a document is the main text, and everything that appears in your document following the title is part of the body.

### Body tags

The tags that follow all have some affect on the body text, and they all lie between the <BODY> and </BODY> tags.

**Headings:** You can use up to six levels of headings for your body text in HTML, and these are numbered 1 (the most important heading) to 6. In fact, few documents need more

119

than three levels, so this allocation is generous. The heading levels are distinguished by using large or bolder type, and the tag contains the level number. For example <H1> is a level 1 heading and <H3> is a level three heading.

- You should not use headings out of sequence. A level-1 heading should be followed by either another level-1 heading or by a level-2 heading, not by any other level

**Paragraphs:** Body text is divided into paragraphs, and these paragraphs can be as long or as short as you like. Each time you use the paragraph tag <P> your browser will take a new paragraph. Note that line ends are not important, a browser will use whatever line length is permitted by the width of its window. The items that are called whitespace, such as spaces, new-line characters, carriage return characters and tabs, are all reduced to a single space in HTML.

- This makes it important to look at your HTML text using a browser if you have prepared the text in a word processor or any other WYSIWYG editor.

- You might want to put in the tags <P></P> to create a blank line for spacing purposes.

You can include an alignment attribute within a paragraph tag, using the word ALIGN along with LEFT, CENTER or RIGHT. Note that browsers will ignore the word CENTRE and recognise only the US form of the word. You seldom need to use LEFT, because this is the default, but for centring:

<P ALIGN=CENTER> will centre the text that lies between this tag and the ending tag of </P>. Note the space between P and ALIGN, but no space either side of the = sign.

**Lists**

A very common feature of a document is a list, often used as an index. HTML supports the use of three main list types, bulleted, numbered and definition lists. As we have seen earlier, a definition list consists of two parts per item, such as a word and its definition (hence the name).

Bulleted lists are used where the order of items is not important — you are being asked to take notice of each item equally. A numbered list should be used when the items are in order of importance.

A **bulleted list** has to be started with the <UL> tag, with UL meaning unnumbered list. Each item on the list must then start with <LI>, but you do not need a corresponding </LI> to end an item. You must, however, have the </UL> tag at the end of the complete list. For example, the HTML codes:

```
<UL>
<LI> memory
<LI> motherboards
<LI> processors
</UL>
```

will, when the code is viewed by a browser, appear as:

• memory

• motherboards

• processors

An item in a list does not need to be short or contained in a single line or even a single paragraph. If you use more than one paragraph, remember to use the <P> and </P> tags to indicate the additional paragraphs.

A **numbered list** is created in a way that is almost identical except it uses <OL> instead of <UL>. The OL means ordered list, emphasising that items are in order of importance. The same <LI> tag is used for each item.

A **definition list** uses the tag <DL> to introduce the list, and each items will have two parts, the definition *term* (a word or phrase) and a definition *definition* (the explanation of the

word or phrase. These are distinguished by using the tags
<DT> for the definition term and <DD> for the definition
definition.

- Browsers use these tags to print the definition term on
  one line, and the definition definition on a new line and
  indented. You can use more than one paragraph for
  either.

- A COMPACT attribute can be used when the two parts
  of an item are both very short.

You can nest lists, meaning that you can have one list within
another. You need to be certain that you close each list
correctly, starting with the innermost list, so that you should
try to avoid excessive nesting.

For example:

```
<UL>
<LI> Computer components for upgrading
<UL>
<LI> Motherboards
<LI> Processors
<LI> Memory
</UL>
<LI> Software
<UL>
<LI> Word for Windows
<LI> Excel
</UL>
</UL>
```

This will be displayed by a browser as

- Computer components for upgrading
-    Motherboards
-    Processors
-    Memory
- Software

- Word for Windows
- Excel

**Monospaced text** : this is text in a font that uses the same width for each character. HTML calls this type of text preformatted, and uses the tag <PRE> to identify it.

When this tag is used, any spaces, tab characters and newline characters are not substituted. Any spaces that you put into your text between the <PRE> tags will be displayed with its spaces intact. This is useful for simple tables, and it was intended originally for typing computer program listings. It is not particularly important for the type of Web page you are likely to want to use. There is a WIDTH attribute that can be added to specify the maximum number of characters per line.

- If you use a monospaced section of text avoid placing any tags other than hyperlinks into this section

**Quotations:** The convention for quoting text that is of more than a few lines is to show this as a block with indents each side. This is done by using the <BLOCKQUOTE> tag to contain the text.

**Addresses:** An address will, of necessity contain several short lines, and if you used the <P> tag for each the lines would be too widely separated. HTML copes with this by using the <BR> tag to cause a line break without additional line spacing. The <BR> tag is placed at the end of each line, and there is no </BR> tag. For example:

Mr. J. Hoffnung,<BR>
126 The Rushes,<BR>
Picturedrome, W7<BR>

will ensure that the lines are correctly viewed in the browser.

**Horizontal lines:** These are produced by using the <HR> tag containing attributes that describe the line size

## Web site construction simplified

(thickness) and width. The width is quoted as a percentage figure, placed between quotes, of the total viewing width, so that the effect is correct for differing sizes of viewing windows.

If you use <HR> with no attributes, the line will be of default thickness and will extend across the full width. To control thickness and width, add the attributes SIZE= and WIDTH=. For example, you can use a command such as:

<HR SIZE=3 WIDTH="50%">

## Text character effects

In text that you prepare using a word processor, you are accustomed to emphasising words or even single characters by using bold or italic printer, possibly by underlining. We need to know how this is done in HTML and the problem is that HTML can use either of two methods, logical styles or physical styles.

The difference is becoming less important. When you use a physical style, you force the browser to use a particular effect. When you use a logical style, you specify an emphasis, but the browser will interpret that in the way it is set up to do. The differences were important in the days when a large number of different browsers were in use, but less so now that a substantial majority of users have Internet Explorer.

The heading tags are logical tags. When you specify a heading as <H2> it is up to your browser to determine what this will look like on the screen. If you had defined the text as 18-point bold Century Schoolbook then the browser would have to try to use it, and would have to make some substitution if it did not have this particular font.

- Logical styles require rather less effort, and you should use them unless you have some particular reason for using the physical styles. The important thing is not to mix the two, because you might easily end up with a browser displaying sections that are intended to be of quite different appearance but which are not.

**Logical styles list**

**<DFN>** is used for a definition of a word, and is usually displayed in italics.

**<EM>** means emphasis and is also displayed in italics by many browsers.

**<CITE>** is used for quoted items such as book titles, and is also usually displayed in italics.

**<CODE>** is reserved for computer program listings, using a monospaced font with a fixed line width.

**<KBD>** is used to distinguish something you are required to type, and is usually displayed in bold.

**<SAMP>** is intended for a set of fixed-width characters.

**<STRONG>** is for heavy emphasis, and this usually means bold.

<VAR> is used for a placeholder, something that you will substitute, like *yournameher*. It is usually shown in italics.

**Physical styles list**

These consist only of bold, italic and monospaced effects.

<B> bold text

<I> italic text

<TT> typewriter text, monospaced.

**Escape Sequences**

Escape sequences, so called because at one time they were signalled by using the character produced by the Esc key, are used for displaying characters that are use for HTML coding or characters, such as foreign accented characters, that are not part of the simple ASCII set.

- One important point about these escape characters is that they must use lower case, you cannot ignore case as you do for other HTML commands.

As we have noted earlier, the characters < , >, and & are used for coding purposes in HTML, so that if you want any of these in ordinary text you must code them by using, respectively, &lt, &gt and &amp. You can also use &quot for quotation marks, but this is not necessary because you can type these directly.

There are other escape sequences that are used to display accented characters, and some of these are illustrated here. Each starts with &, then the character, then the coding for the accent:

&ouml means a lowercase o with an umlaut: ö

&Ntilde means a uppercase N with a tilde: Ñ

&egrave an lowercase e with a grave accent: è

## Links

One of the most important features of a document in HTML is the way that it can include hyperlinks to different sections of text, other pages or documents on other Web sites. Where the HTML codes for such a link occur in a document, a browser will usually use colour and/or underlining to identify the link, and most browsers distinguish between a link that has not been clicked and one that has (a followed link).

When you want to use an item on a page, such as a heading, as a link to another HTML document you identify the linking item as an anchor, using the <A> tag. The starting <A> tag needs to contain the route to the page you want.

For example, suppose you want the word *books* in some piece of text to link to a booklist in the document booklist.htm. The entry in the text that contains the line would have the word books coded as:

<A HREF="booklist.htm">books</A>

This assumes that the file booklist.htm is in the same folder on your Web site as the main index file. If you need a link to a document in a subfolder then you have to specify that subfolder, such as:

<A HREF="Mydata/booklist.htm">books</A>

where the file is in a subfolder called Mydata.

These links that use files in your own Web space are called relative links because you are specifying the path to the linked file relative to the location of the index file. They have the advantage of making your documents easier to access no matter where the folder that contains them is placed. We have emphasised this by pointing out how easily you can check your Web pages if you keep them locally in a folder.

The alternative, used particularly for files that do not belong to you, is to use the *absolute* pathname, which means the complete URL.

You become accustomed to using one type of URL, the http:// type. A URL will includes the type of resource that you want to use, the address of the server, and the location of the file. You can write this in the form (a *syntax*):

type://host.domain.path/ filename

where *type* can be file, ftp, http or several others including gopher, WAIS. news, or telnet. The common ones are file, meaning a file on your own computer, ftp, meaning a file on an FTP server, and http, meaning a file on a World Wide Web server. For example, if you type the line:

# Web site construction simplified

```
<A HREF="http://www.microsoft.com">Microsoft</A>
```

then this would have the effect of marking the word Microsoft as a link to the Web URL for Microsoft.

## Named anchors

A named anchor (bookmark) is used when you want to use an index in your (long) page, so that the reader can quickly move from one section of the page to another. You need first to identify the target, which is often a heading. This is done using the NAME tag. The construction is:

```
<A NAME=name>
```

and you can use whatever you like as a name provided that it is unique — you must not have more than one of this name.

For example, suppose you have the heading:

```
<H3>Motherboard types<H3>
```

and you want this to be the target of a link from an index. You would alter this so that it became:

```
<H3><A NAME="MTHR">Motherboard types</A><H3>
```

so that the name MTHR is now the target name for this heading. You would then create the line by having in the index or table of contents for your page an entry such as:

```
<A.HREF="#MTHR">Motherboards</A>
```

You can also link to a specific section in another document that is contained in the same set

Suppose you want to set a link from our main document called index.htm to a heading called *Electronics* in another document called booklist.htm. The link code in your Index htm file might looks like this:

```
<A HREF="booklist.htm#ELEC">Electronics</A>
```

with the hash mark indicating the reference that appears as a bookmark in the booklist.htm file.

You can then edit the booklist.htm file to put in the target:

<H2>A NAME="ELEC">Electronics List</A></H2>

## Images

At this point, things become complicated. Modern Web browsers can be guaranteed to display images along with text if the images are in a suitable format, which normally means either GIF or JPG. Remember that you should try to avoid placing images into your index page because each image considerably increases the time needed to download your page.

Each image file must be available in your server folder because though the images appear to be in the text, they are saved separately, and unless the browser can find them they will not appear.

• Remember also the complications that can be caused if you use uppercase for your graphics filenames and links to them.

The tag for an image is <IMG SRC=name>, where name means the filename. This filename will have to include a path if the image files are in a subfolder of yous Web site folder.

For example, <IMG SRC="Mydog.gif"> will put in at the cursor position the picture you have specified, using the same size as it was when it was saved.

• Note that the picture title must be placed between quotes

If you want to specify the size of the image, as you normally do, then you must add the attributes of HEIGHT and WIDTH to your IMG SRC tag. The dimensions are in screen pixels, so that unless you can think in these terms you will

# Web site construction simplified

have to use some try and see methods before you get the image size just as you want it. As a rough guide, think of 75 pixels per inch.

For example, you might want to use dimensions of height and width equal to, respectively, 150 and 75 pixels, and this would be coded as:

<IMG SRC="Mydog.gif" HEIGHT="150" WIDTH="75">

- Note the quotes around names and dimensions.

You will also want to align your pictures. The image can be aligned with the text, separated, placed left, centred or right as you please. The default is that the bottom of an image is aligned with the text that follows it.

You can change this by using the ALIGN= attribute along with TOP or CENTER.

For example, the dog photo could have text aligned with the top of the picture by using:

<IMG SRC="Mydog.gif" ALIGN=TOP>

- You can keep an image separate from text by making the image a separate paragraph, placing it between <P> and </P>, and you can also align the image by including attributes like ALIGN=CENTER in the first <P> line.

Another point about images is that you can opt for your browser not to download images, so greatly speeding up Web contacts. You can use HTML code to show a caption in place of a picture if the picture is not downloaded. This is done using the <ALT> tag. For example:

<IMG SRC="Mydog.gif" ALT="Picture of Posy, my dog">

will ensure that either the picture or the caption text will appear, depending on the settings of the browser.

- Remember that if you have turned off picture downloading on your browser you can still obtain pictures by right-clicking on the picture position and selecting *Show Picture*.

## Image links

Images that you have incorporated into your text can be used as hyperlinks as easily as plain text. You have to add the anchor reference into the picture line :

<A HREF="Dogfacts.htm"><IMG SRC="Mydog.gif"></A>

and ensure that there is a target file, Dogfacts.htm in this example, to link to.

When you make a link using a picture like this, the browser will show a blue border around the picture. This border is normally useful as an indicator that the picture is a hyperlink but you can remove it by using BORDER=0 within the ING SRC part of the line.

- BORDER is also used to produce various coloured border effects for pictures.

### Backgrounds

Modern browsers can use an image as a faint background to a page — my own Web site shows a logic diagram of a 486 chip as a background. You have to ensure that whatever you use in this way is faint enough to act as a background rather than competing for attention with the main text or pictures in the foreground. If the image is smaller than is needed to fill the page it will be tiled in the way that is familiar from Windows wallpaper.

The background is added by adding a BACKGROUND attribute to the <BODY> tag. For example:

<BODY BACKGROUND="80486.gif">

is the line I use for my Web page.

131

# Web site construction simplified

You can also opt to control both background and foreground colours. The browser default is black text on a white or grey background. Normally, this is sufficient for easy reading, and one of the problems of making changes in colours is to ensure that the results are still readable when you view with a browser. Remember that a fair percentage of the male population is colour-blind to some extent so that some colour combinations will be totally unreadable for these people.

Colours are controlled by using other attributes within the <BODY> tag. The trouble is that the system that is normally used depends on the use of numbers to represent colours, and this is by no means simple. If you are content to use the old system of sixteen colours, you can get away with using these names as attributes, so that:

```
<BODY BGCOLOR="black" TEXT="#white" LINK="red">
```

will ensure that your browser uses a black background, white text and red hyperlinks.

The other method is to type a six-digit number for each colour. Any colour can be analysed in terms of a mixture of red, green and blue light, so that each colour you can display has a unique RGB value. If we represent the amount of each of these primary colours as a number with two digits, then we can combine the digits to form the six-digit code for the colour we want. However, the numbers are quoted in scale of sixteen (hexadecimal), so that it is by no means easy to specify a colour unless you have software that can provide the colour code for any colour that you click in a display.

## Thumbnails

A thumbnail is a small image that downloads rapidly to give you some clue about the picture. Clicking on this thumbnail will then download the full-size picture. This is a useful method that allows your index page to be full of small pictures that a viewer can see in detail if required, but without using the excessive download time that would be needed if each full-size image were downloaded. The larger image is referred to as an *external image*.

The form of the code that you need to use for this is:

<A HREF="Main.gif"><IMG SRC="Thumbnail.gif"></A>

The browser page will display the Thumbnail.gif small image and you can click on it to download and open the Mail.gif file.

**Tables**

Table construction is by far the most tedious part of working in HTML, and we can be thankful that editors are available to make the task easier. For that reason, the subject is not covered in detail here, because you are much more likely to look at the HTML for checking purposes rather than for the purpose of creating a table from scratch.

The elements of a table include heads, the key to the contents of rows and columns, along with the columns and rows themselves and the cells that are used to hold information for each column and row position.

A table will start with the <TABLE> tag, which can use a variety of attributes to show the size of the table, cell spacing and padding and so on. The <TH> tag is used to define headers. This is followed by an entry for each cell, working across left to right in each row and down the rows. Each row starts with a <TR> tag, and for each cell in the row the entry is of the form:

<TD WIDTH="33%" VALIGN="TOP">

<P ALIGN="JUSTIFY">Able</TD>

where the TD entry describes the cell, and the <P entry indicates the text in the cell.

## Web site construction simplified

- All of these defining tags must be placed between the <TABLE> and </TABLE> tags .

## Forms

If you have looked at some of the more advanced templates of FrontPage Express you will have seen one that creates forms. These forms are intended to enable a user to return information to a Web server file for some action by you. For example, you might want to collect the e-mail addresses for people who were interested in some aspect of your Web site — the commercial possibilities are endless.

The aim of all this will be to add information to a database, and that's where HTML gives out, because this information handling has to be done by some program written for the purpose. You may find that your server can provide lines of code that can be added to your page that will, with some modifications, do what you want, but if nothing is available there is not much you can do about it unless you see a tip in a book or magazine.

# Appendix

## A hit counter

The following line of code is suggested by Global as a way of implementing a hit counter, and the result can be seen on my page.

You need to add the line, exactly as shown but with your own email address name in place of the *username* item.

```
<p><font size="6"><strong>You are visitor
number</strong></font><strong>
<img src="/cgi-bin/Count.cgi?ft=9|frgb=69;139;50|tr=0|
trgb=0;0;0|wxh=15;20|md=6|dd=A|st=5|sh=1|
df=username.dat"
align="absmiddle"> </strong></p>
```

Note that this was originally typed as one long line, and you should not press the Return key in the course of it.

When you view the files locally, you will see a small icon in the place indicated by the text, but when the file is uploaded and you browse the Web site, the hit count will display.

# Web site construction simplified

# INDEX

3D effects, table ............... 35

absolute links ........... **74, 127**
abstract ........................... **110**
accented letters ............. **4, 42**
activate site ...................... **95**
activate your Web space .... **9**
advice, Alta Vista ........... **109**
aims and objectives .......... **13**
align picture ............. **32, 130**
alignment attribute ......... **120**
alignment icons ................ **27**
alignment of image .......... **64**
alignment, cells ................ **62**
alignment, line ................. **42**
Alta Vista ...................... **107**
alternate ........................... **45**
Amaya ........................ **7, 64**
Amaya HTML display ..... **65**
analysis ............................ **80**
anchor ............................ **126**
anchor, AOLpress ........... **57**
angle brackets ............ **5, 116**
anonymous FTP ............... **93**
AOLpress ..................... **7, 51**
ASCII code ........................ **4**
ASCII plain text ............. **116**
ASCII text ........................ **85**
attributes ........................ **117**
Authoring Wizard ............. **7**

background ..................... **131**
background, AOLpress .... **56**
background sound ............ **40**
background, table ............. **35**
backslash mark .................. **2**
blank line ...................... **120**
blue hyperlinks ................ **23**

body text ........................ **119**
bold .................................. **28**
bookmarked section ......... **23**
bookmarking .................... **29**
border colours .................. **37**
break a line ...................... **41**
browse for files ................ **53**
browsing file display ........ **93**
browsing, Amaya .............. **65**
bulleted list .............. **24, 121**
bullets and numbering menu
...................................... **39**
buttons ............................. **87**

CAD ................................. **16**
caption ........................... **130**
cell padding ..................... **35**
cell properties .................. **37**
cell size ........................... **33**
cell spacing ...................... **35**
cell span .......................... **38**
Cetus Notepad .................. **20**
change font size ............... **28**
change picture size ........... **63**
character styles, AOLpress
...................................... **59**
checking your entry ....... **114**
codings .............................. **5**
colour background ........... **36**
colour, line ...................... **42**
columns of text ................ **32**
comment, AOLpress ......... **56**
comments .......................... **43**
compact files ..................... **4**
compressing files ............... **4**
confirmation form ............. **75**
contact information ........... **25**
convention, filename ........ **90**

137

# Web site construction simplified

convert ASCII to HTML ... **8**
convert HTML to text files **8**
CorelDraw! 4.0 .............. **17**
corner handle .................. **63**
corner handles ................. **32**
create page in AOLpress.. **54**
creating HTML ................. **6**
custom background, cell .. **38**
cut/copy ASCII ............... **20**

definition list ............ **24, 121**
definition, definition list .. **60**
delete files on Web site.... **10**
document head ............... **117**
dotted blue underlining .... **23**
download .......................... **4**
drag and drop files .......... **10**
drag folders and files ....... **97**
drop caps ........................ **47**
drop-down box ............... **87**
dual-window display ........ **97**

editing losses, JPG ........... **15**
elements of document .... **116**
elements of table ........... **133**
e-mail address ................. **25**
embedding ........................ **73**
emphasis ........................... **28**
ending tag ....................... **116**
escape sequences ... **116, 125**
Explorer browser .............. **8**

fanaticism ........................ **14**
file locations .................... **73**
File Transfer Protocol **10, 91**
filling in detail ................. **13**
Font menu ........................ **28**
font sizes ......................... **47**
Form Page Wizard .......... **77**
form, entering URL ....... **109**

format a paragraph ........... **27**
forms ............................. **134**
free software .................... **19**
FrontPage Express ....... **6, 19**
FTP ............................ **10, 91**
FTP Explorer ................. **102**
FTP software ................... **10**
fully justified text ........... **27**

GIF format ...................... **15**
Global Internet .................. **1**
grammar checking ............. **8**
graphic in cell ................. **34**
graphical material ............ **15**
graphics handling, Word .. **50**

handle ............................. **63**
handles ............................ **32**
header cells ..................... **62**
Help files ........................... **7**
History list ....................... **53**
hit counter ................ **97, 135**
home page, AOLpress ...... **52**
horizontal line ................. **42**
horizontal line, Amaya ..... **68**
horizontal lines .............. **123**
HotDog ....................... **7, 84**
HTML .............................. **4**
HTML editor ............... **6, 83**
HTML guide .................. **115**
HTTP .............................. **92**
hyperlink ...................... **3, 18**
hyperlink to bookmark ..... **29**
hyperlinks ................ **11, 126**
hyperlinks to other pages.. **30**

icons, character formatting
..................................... **67**
icons, indentation ............. **28**
icons. AOLpress .............. **55**

image links...................... 131
images ............................ 129
images, AOLpress............ 62
import file ........................ 22
import formatted text ....... 20
import image, AOLpress . 63
import text.................. **79, 85**
indent text ........................ 28
index page.......................... 5
*index.htm*............................. 9
insert caption.................... 34
insert column ................... 34
insert graphical image...... 31
insert row ......................... 34
insert symbol.................... 42
internal links .................... 25
IP (Information Provider) .. 1
italic ................................. 28
item, definition list........... 60

Java language............... **1, 43**
JPG format ....................... 15

keywords........................ **108**

layout, cell......................... 38
layout, table...................... 35
levels of headings .......... **119**
line spacing, Amaya......... 68
link to other site ............... 31
linking .............................. 73
links................................ **126**
links, AOLpress .............. 57
links to graphics.............. 17
links, Amaya .................... 70
list.......................... **14, 120**
list, AOLpress ................. 59
local folder ....................... 73
location line ..................... 53
logical styles .................. **124**

logical styles list ............ **125**
look at files locally .............8
low-cost way......................8
lower case ........................89
lower-case lettering ............9
Lycos ............................ **107**

main file............................9
main headings...................12
main sections, index page.23
main text headings............13
maintaining site ..............**6, 9**
margins ............................41
mathematical work ..........64
menu line, FPE .................21
merge cells........................61
meta-tags........................ **110**
minimum width, cell........38
minimum width, table.......35
monospaced font........ **58, 83**
monospaced text ............ **123**

named anchor ................ **128**
nest lists ......................... **122**
Net Creations PostMaster
    .................................. **111**
new paragraph .................27
newline ............................41
normal page option...........77
normal style ......................28
numbered list .......... **24, 121**
outlining Web page ..........12

page numbering ................48
page title ..........................24
Paint Shop Pro .................17
painting package...............16
paper copy ........................14
paragraphs...................... **120**
password ..........................93

# Web site construction simplified

paste in text ....................... **33**
path............................... **2**
Personal Home Page Wizard
................................ **23**
photographs...................... **15**
physical styles ................ **124**
physical styles list .......... **125**
picture, Amaya................. **69**
pictures............................ **15**
plain text .......................... **80**
planning .......................... **5**
preformatted text............ **123**
presentation options ......... **24**
print preview, Word........... **8**
programming ability .......... **1**

quoting text .................... **123**

range, font sizes ............... **28**
read critically ................... **13**
ready-made template........ **22**
refresh display................ **100**
relative links................... **127**
relative reference ............. **74**
remove formatting ........... **39**
repetition, Marquee.......... **45**
reply form ........................ **87**
re-position picture............ **63**
right-hand mouse button,
    Amaya ......................... **66**
robot icon ......................... **43**

Sausage Software.............. **84**
Save As uploading ........... **90**
scanner ............................ **15**
script.............................. **44**
scroll.............................. **45**
Scrolling Marquee ........... **44**
search actions.................. **114**
search agencies ............. **107**

search engines................ **107**
sections of data ................ **12**
select a table, AOLpress ... **62**
server ................................ **3**
set of headings ................. **11**
shareware ........................ **19**
Shift key, picture shape .... **63**
*Show picture* option.......... **16**
single page ....................... **11**
site maintenance ............ **100**
site map............................ **100**
size of files....................... **15**
skeleton page .................... **26**
skeleton table .................... **61**
slash mark ...................... **116**
slide.................................. **45**
SmartSuite ........................ **6**
software, FTP .................... **92**
sound................................ **18**
special effects .................... **6**
spell-checking.................... **7**
spelling checker ... **20, 64, 79**
spelling checker, AOLpress
    ...................................... **55**
split up into pages............. **12**
start design....................... **12**
start index page................. **22**
styles................................ **28**
styles, AOLpress .............. **58**
subfolder ......................... **73**
sub-headings ..................... **13**
Submit-It! ...................... **111**
survey form....................... **77**
symbol ............................. **42**
synopsis .......................... **12**

table ................................ **14**
table alterations................. **34**
table construction .......... **133**
table properties ................ **35**

table, Amaya .................... **68**
table, AOLpress ............... **60**
tables .............................. **32**
tag list............................ **119**
tags ............................... **116**
template.......................... **20**
templates, other ............... **75**
terms............................... **2**
Terrapin FTP.................... **96**
text box .......................... **87**
text boxes ........................ **49**
text colour, AOLpress...... **56**
text editing, AOLpress..... **55**
text editor .......................... **3**
text to Web converters ..... **80**
text, Amaya...................... **66**
Text2Web ........................ **80**
thickness, line ................. **42**
thumbnail ....................... **132**
ToolTips............................ **4**
two dots symbol............... **53**
type title, AOLpress......... **54**
typing text, table cells ...... **61**

underlining....................... **28**
Unix .............................. **3, 89**
unsupported features, Word
    ...................................... **46**
upload.............................. **3**
uploading ..................... **9, 89**

uploading files .................... **5**
URL ...................... **3, 24, 92**
user name.........................**93**

video .................................**18**
view HTML codes............**25**
views, in Web page ..........**14**

watermark ........................**40**
Web Authoring, Word......**46**
Web page ..........................**11**
Web Publishing Wizard....**94**
Web sites .............................**1**
Web software....................**19**
WebBot...................... **22, 76**
whitespace ..................... **120**
width, line ........................**42**
Word ............................ **4, 45**
Word 8.0 .............................**7**
Word 97 ...................... **7, 78**
word processor ...................**3**
Word tables......................**49**
words in index page..........**12**
WPWIZ.EXE....................**94**
WS_FTP ....................... **103**
WYSIWYG editor..............**6**
WYSIWYG Web page
    software .......................**20**

zip file............................ **102**

# Web site construction simplified

NOTES

# Web site construction simplified

NOTES